See Steve See

Mini Memoirs with
Laughs and Life Lessons

Steve Hoberman

Technics Publications
SEDONA, ARIZONA

115 Linda Vista, Sedona, AZ 86336 USA
https://www.TechnicsPub.com

Edited by Sadie Hoberman and Jamie Hoberman

Cover design by Lorena Molinari
Illustrations by Joseph Shepherd

All rights reserved. No part of this book may be reproduced or transmitted in any form or by any means, electronic or mechanical, including photocopying, recording, or by any information storage and retrieval system, without written permission from the publisher, except for brief quotations in a review.

The authors and publisher have taken care in the preparation of this book, but make no expressed or implied warranty of any kind and assume no responsibility for errors or omissions. No liability is assumed for incidental or consequential damages in connection with or arising out of the use of the information or programs contained herein.

All trade and product names are trademarks, registered trademarks, or service marks of their respective companies and are the property of their respective holders and should be treated as such.

Without in any way limiting the author's exclusive rights under copyright, any use of this publication to "train" generative artificial intelligence (AI) technologies to generate text is expressly prohibited. The author reserves all rights to license uses of this work for generative AI training and the development of machine learning language models.

First Printing 2025
Copyright © 2025 by Steve Hoberman

ISBN, print ed.	9781634626408 (softcover)
ISBN, print ed.	9781634626415 (hardcover)
ISBN, Kindle ed.	9781634625876
ISBN, PDF ed.	9781634625883

Library of Congress Control Number: 2024948440

To the three wonderful girls that are my world.

Contents

Introduction _____ 5

2019

January _____ 7
February _____ 11
March _____ 13
April _____ 15
May _____ 17
June _____ 19
July _____ 21
August _____ 23
September _____ 27
October _____ 29
November _____ 31
December _____ 33

2020

January _____ 37
February _____ 41
March _____ 45
April _____ 47
May _____ 49
June _____ 51
July _____ 53
August _____ 55
September _____ 57
October _____ 59
November _____ 63
December _____ 65

2021

January	67
February	69
March	73
April	75
May	77
June	81
July	83
August	85
September	87
October	89
November	91
December	93

2022

January	95
February	97
March	99
April	101
May	103
June	105
July	107
August	111
September	113
October	115
November	119
December	121

2023

January	123
February	125
March	127
April	131
May	133
June	135
July	139

August _____ 143
September _____ 147
October _____ 151
November _____ 155
December _____ 157

2024

January _____ 161
February _____ 165
March _____ 169
April _____ 171
May _____ 175
June _____ 179
July _____ 181
August _____ 185
September _____ 187
October _____ 191
November _____ 193
December _____ 195

Life Tactics

What works _____ 199
Do "to do" _____ 201
Play the crane game _____ 209
Identify your gifts _____ 213
Stretch _____ 215
Learn then leverage _____ 221
Ask _____ 225
Go veg _____ 227
Travel _____ 229
Act like the expert _____ 231
Laugh often _____ 235

Conclusion _____ 239

Introduction

What do sandcastles, road trips, and penguins have in common? They're just a few of the many topics in this collection of entertaining and reflective short stories from six years of my life.

As a data management professional, I have been consulting, training, and writing about data since 1990. For over 20 years, I have been sending out a monthly newsletter with currently more than 25,000 subscribers (join us at https://technicspub.com/SeeSteveSee). The newsletter covers technology and ends with me sharing a personal story.

After years of requests from newsletter subscribers, I turned six years of stories (2019 to 2025) into a book. These 72 short memoirs appear chronologically to present a unique picture of how we change and how world events impact our lives.

The stories are organized by month within year, and align with the month when I sent out the newsletter. For example, I might share a Halloween story in November and a July 4th story in August. Also, I chose six years of stories instead of

20 to keep it entertaining and not to create a doorstop or sleep aid.

These six years definitely contained some goodies, including Covid, wars, inflation, AI, and the final episode of Game of Thrones. At a personal level, I turned 50, our family moved from New Jersey to Arizona, and our two daughters started college, leaving my wife and me as "empty nesters."

Ten themes thread through the stories and appear in the last chapter as life tactics. Use these proven techniques to get more out of your days.

Whether looking for a lighthearted read or seeking inspiration, I hope this book makes you smile, reflect, and grow.

Ready? Let's go!

2019

January

I consider myself an expert in the airport security process. While waiting in the security line, I take everything out of my pockets, remove all liquids, and have my laptop in hand ready to be placed in a security bin—if you've been on a plane at least once in the last 15 years, you know the drill. If there are multiple security lines to choose from, I quickly analyze each line. Not just by how many people are in each line, but I use a point system: people who look like frequent flyers get one point, people with lots of odd-shaped carry-on luggage get two points, families get two points for each member—and I choose the line with the lowest point score, just like mini-golf.

If you've ever seen the movie 'Up in the Air,' at times, I can make George Clooney look like a first-time traveler.

Last week was not one of these times, though. My family and I were going through airport security, coming home after a week abroad. Between my wife, our two daughters, and I, we probably filled close to 15 security bins. In addition, most of our luggage took the form of either white garbage bags (don't ask) or large glitzy shopping bags from various airport stores. A word of advice: never get to the airport too early with anyone who likes to shop.

About half of our bags were selected for additional screening, mostly due to these bags containing electronics and liquids that were accidentally not removed. The security person doing the additional screening was very patient, even after we found an entire makeup container filled with liquids and lotions belonging to my younger daughter. As I quickly started removing all of the bottles and tubes for airport scanning, I realized a tube of her toothpaste exploded at some point during our travels, creating a thick sticky goo on most of the container's belongings.

Finally, after another 10 minutes of pure airport security agony, my family and I made it through.

As my blood pressure started returning to normal, I watched in horror as my family sprinted into the nearest duty-free shop for a final round of shopping before boarding the plane.

February

What's good about turning 50? I recently turned the "Big 5-0," and woke up the morning of my birthday hungry for inspiration.

My younger daughter greeted me with, "Well, now you're halfway over the rainbow." I'm not sure what she meant by this, but her evil chuckle probably meant I should not be inspired. My older daughter handed me a card, and my hope for inspiration quickly faded when the only words scribbled inside were "Happy Birthday" and then she vanished back into her phone.

My wife offered me some personal training sessions at the gym as a birthday present instead of working out with weights in the basement. She then added, "Now that you're 50, maybe you should start lifting weights the right way so you don't hurt yourself." Throughout the day, friends and family members called and reinforced the thoughts in my head that 50 is the beginning of getting old.

The only inspiration I found during my birthday came from my dog, Daisy. Daisy rushed to me in the morning to be petted and demanded food and attention throughout the day, like she does every day. She didn't even notice I turned 50.

March

We have six pets: a dog, four chickens, and a fish. Fish make great pets…just replace the water every once in a while and feed them…they don't need to be walked three times a day like our dog or have their pens cleaned like our chickens.

Our older daughter started our fish collection many years ago by "winning" a fish at the school carnival. After spending over $100 on a fish tank, filter, and a neon castle and treasure chest for the fish to swim around, I became convinced that "winning" was not the right word.

Over the years, fish "move on" and new fish took their place...such is life. As our kids got older, we stopped replenishing the fish that moved on. As of five years ago, we were down to just one fish remaining and expected that fish to "move on" shortly as well. However, this fish did not "move on." Instead, this fish stayed and stayed, and is still happily swimming today. It must be close to ten years old!

Due to an automatic fish food feeder (one of the best inventions of our time), we no longer needed to visit the fish every day. Our daughter eventually lost interest and since the water now rarely gets replaced, the fish tank is a very dark inky green and sometimes we have to look really hard to see if there is something in there still swimming...but he is (or she is...).

I imagine decades from now, rocking in a chair on the porch, reading a good data modeling book, and hearing that fish filter hum in the background as that stubborn fish swims on.

April

Ever see a chicken smile? Finally, after a brutal winter here in New Jersey, last week was a sign that spring is finally challenging Old Man Winter, as the thick covering of snow melted to mounds of snow dotting our yard, revealing the grass underneath. Temperatures were warmer, too, so we opened the door to the coop to let our four chickens scratch in the grass and spread out a bit in our yard.

Close to our house is a section of grass that had been reduced to dirt years ago (thanks to our chickens). The sun was warming this area, so the chickens decided to take a dust bath. A dust bath is when a chicken rolls in the dirt, flapping their wings, like a dog rolling playfully on the ground.

All four of them scratched, rolled, and flung dirt at each other, creating a cloud of dust as they enjoyed the warm afternoon sun and the beginning of the spring season.

I didn't get close enough to see if they were actually smiling…but I knew they were.

May

Our 16-year-old daughter goes to parties—parties with boys. It used to be so much simpler when "boys were gross" and playdates were girls only.

My wife and I feel slightly more in control when the parties are at our house, like the party our daughter hosted this past Saturday. If I counted correctly, as the kids awkwardly greeted us before scurrying into the basement, the official "no parents zone," there were three girls and 12 boys—12 boys! How can there be 12 boys over our house?

My wife and I tried to console each other that girls mature quicker than boys, and this was confirmed when we saw one of the boys come upstairs looking for a place to hide. Our daughter and her friends decided to play "hide and seek," where one person hides and everyone else tries to find that person. Our entire house became a haven for hiders (our house has some great hiding spots), as footsteps and laughing were heard above us and in the rooms around us.

After several hours of playing hide and seek, one of the boys found a hiding spot that was too good. The rest of the party eventually gave up looking for him and returned to the basement to continue their party antics. Some time later, I heard a creaking of a door and light footsteps as the boy who was hiding quietly made his way back into the basement to join the party.

I learned two lessons from this evening—you're never too old to play "hide and seek," and if you are the one hiding, hide in a place where people can find you!

June

One of the best places to spend Memorial Day, the unofficial start of summer, is at the Jersey Shore. Nearby is a boardwalk with lots of amusement rides and indoor games, and faced with a cold rainy Sunday, our family decided to stick with the indoor games.

The kids play games to win tickets and then cash in the tickets for prizes. When I was a kid, I remember spending dimes to win tickets for fairly decent prices—these days, it's

$1 and $5 bills. After spending probably $20 or $30, you've earned enough tickets to "win" a plastic kazoo or a small rubber spider.

Our younger daughter put $5 into a game where you shoot a coin at an existing pile of coins sliding back and forth, intending to knock some of these coins into a chute. Coins get traded for tickets, and tickets are traded for cheap plastic and rubber prizes. She had knocked quite a few coins into the chute, but no coins came out—they appeared to be clogged somewhere in the machine.

I called over a game attendant, who opened up the machine. Inside was a treasure chest of coins, probably from dozens of kids who had not claimed their winnings. The attendant, not knowing (or caring) if our daughter had won all of these coins, filled a large container to the top with these coins and handed the heavy treasure to her. It made her day.

She probably could have exchanged this treasure chest of coins for enough tickets to win a tin lunchbox or a large plastic dinosaur, but she kept the coins instead. She felt the value of the coins was worth much more than anything the prize desk could offer.

Sometimes, the means are more important than the end.

July

"Stop picking on her!"

You can imagine a frustrated parent yelling this phrase to an unruly child. But what about to an unruly chicken?

Several weeks ago, a chicken in our flock of four injured her wing. We felt sorry for this chicken, but Googling "broken chicken wings" brought back not just savory recipes and fast food restaurants, but also reassuring articles that chicken wings can heal on their own. Our family felt compassion for this injured chicken, and we anticipated the rest of the flock to also take care of "one of their own."

We were therefore shocked when we witnessed the other chickens pecking the injured chicken. They wanted to kill this injured chicken! In fact, one of these chicken bullies repeatedly jumped high in the air and landed on the injured chicken's back—it could have been a scene from *The Matrix*.

After putting bacitracin on the poor chicken's wounds from being pecked, we separated this chicken from the flock. We bought her a shiny new coop from Amazon. I won't say how much this new coop costs, but I will say you could have bought over 25 chickens at the local supermarket for the cost of this new coop! And this is for ONE chicken…an injured chicken!

We could not leave her alone for too long, so we took her with us on a number of long drives. I don't know how many cars cruise the New Jersey highways with a noisy family, a smelly dog, and an injured chicken, but there is now at least one.

The injured chicken very easily adapted to her new flock (us). We were on a road trip last week and the injured chicken "talked" to us the whole time. I couldn't get her to stop clucking…just like the rest of my flock.

August

You can teach your kids how to play football or ride a bike—but confidence, that can be difficult to teach. We want our kids to boldly take on the world. Our younger daughter often needs a confidence booster.

Last week, for example, she and I rented a wave runner, which is like a motorcycle that rides on water. I drove the wave runner initially while she rode on back. She did not trust herself to drive this watercraft. I eventually stopped the wave runner in the middle of the bay, turned off the engine, and insisted we switch so she could at least drive for a few minutes.

She reluctantly switched places with me and slowly took the handles, gently pressing down on the acceleration. The wave runner lurched forward. She laughed (it was a nervous laugh), pressed the acceleration some more, and we jumped forward at a quicker pace. As she boosted the speed of the watercraft, I pictured her confidence boosting too, and I smiled.

She continued pressing on the acceleration, 30 miles per hour, 40 miles per hour, 50 miles per hour…

She started aiming for the waves and wakes of nearby boats. Her nervous laugh transformed into a wild (almost evil) laugh. She started making sharp turns at over 50 miles per hour. I held on tight to her life jacket…but it was not tight enough.

In what seemed like slow motion, I lost my grip on her life jacket and flew off the back of the wave runner.

I always imagined the soft landing of falling into water, but I realized (and too late) that when traveling near the speed of light, landing on water is no different from landing on cement! I rolled, cracked a rib, and lost my designer Danish glasses somewhere under the surf.

As I slowly regained consciousness, in the distance I heard that wild laugh from our daughter and watched her briefly turn around to make sure I was still alive before zooming off towards the horizon.

As I write this and wash down my prescription painkiller with a glass of water, I realize that was the last confidence lesson I'm giving her.

September

I love auctions. You can win a complete dining room set for $5, or get caught up in the bidding frenzy and wind up with some abstract artwork for $500.

Once a year, the town we live in auctions hundreds of items that are donated by residents to benefit our volunteer fire department, including furniture, collectibles, clothes, lawnmowers, artwork, cars, boats, and more.

This year's auction took place last Saturday. At 8 am, I registered and received a bidding number which I gave to my wife, and we entered the large crowded auction tent. She sat with a friend and I found a seat about five rows ahead.

I found it enjoyable to see how much people were bidding, and one item in particular was this old small table—the bidding started at $20 and quickly went up very high. I could not believe someone would pay that much for an old table, but my thoughts were interrupted when the auctioneer called the winning bidder's number and it sounded familiar. Our number! I turned around to see my wife smiling. This old table is now in our family room.

There were also items for sale during the event, and our younger daughter went off with her friends to do some shopping. She came back with a box of purchases, including some artwork. I took a small oil painting out of her box and recognized it right away—it was actually a painting we donated to the auction!

I tell myself that buying expensive old tables and items that we've donated benefits the fire department. Next year, though, I think I will hold the bidding number!

October

A couple of things are high on my "hate to do" list—going to the dentist, getting a haircut, mall shopping during the holidays, and attending funerals.

This past weekend, we went to a funeral for the father of one of our friends. We knew a bit about the father from conversations over the years with our friends. He was a famous nuclear physicist.

As each of his children came up to speak about their dad, they glossed over his successful career and spent their eulogy time speaking about "small" things. I was curious about his inventions, yet his older son instead shared a story that when he was little, his dad bought him an ice cream cone even after he misbehaved. I wanted to know about the books he had written, yet his daughter talked about working on a particular wood project together. What about his patents? Not mentioned—instead, his younger son talked about fixing car brakes with his dad.

I wonder if this physicist would have imagined that what most likely appeared at the time as non-monumental interactions with his family, would be remembered by those he loved most more than his career accomplishments.

Makes you think.

November

Yesterday, a large black bear made its way across our yard, close to our house and chicken coop. I had never seen a black bear up this close before (not even in a zoo), and was glad we were all inside until I heard barking and realized our little dog Daisy was outside.

She wasn't barking to come inside—she was barking at the bear. The bear continued to walk at its same pace as Daisy circled it and continued to bark viciously. Daisy going after the bear looked like a mouse going after a cat. We screamed to Daisy to come back inside, but she was intent on protecting the property and the chickens and would not leave the bear alone until it disappeared into the brush.

My wife ran out and grabbed Daisy and brought her inside, but the truth was it might have been the bear that needed protecting.

It must be nice not to be aware of your own size or limits.

December

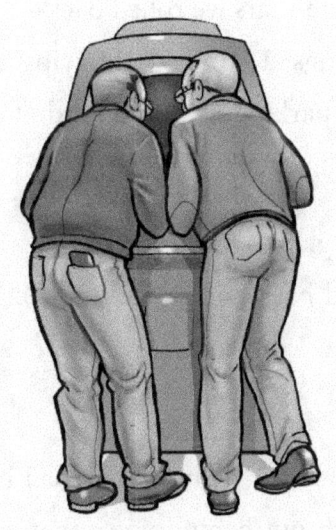

My friend and I grew up together, and although we live on opposite ends of the country today, we try to stay in touch.

Last week, he was on the East Coast, so we met at an arcade filled with vintage video games. After playing a few rounds of Tempest and Galaga, we both started feeding quarters into this 1980s karate game. We worked as a team and with the right combination of moving the joystick and pushing the buttons, our 1980s-resolution karate characters kicked and jumped and punched the bad guys, with the goal of rescuing the princess.

The world around us vanished as we worked together to defeat the ax throwers, black belts, and these scary guys with baseball bats. It seemed like the more quarters we fed the machine, the more years we rolled back—I forgot about my afternoon meetings, I stopped worrying about whether I parked in a legal parking spot, and I didn't even think about my iPhone and the emails piling up.

In fact, I quickly glanced away from the screen at my friend, and then glanced back and saw my reflection on the video game screen and confirmed—we were two 12-year-olds again.

"Hurry up, hit the guy with the baseball bat," followed by "Got him…watch out behind you—that guy has an ax…" Our pre-puberty high-pitched voices filled the air as we advanced from one level to the next…until we reached the final level. The princess was at one end of a dimly lit cave surrounded by a group of thugs, and my friend and I were at the other end, ready for battle.

We attacked the bad guys, one by one, until only three of us remained: the princess, me, and my friend. Triumphant music played, and just when we thought the game was over, a message appeared that we must fight each other for the princess. We were both surprised since we worked as a team the whole journey. But before my friend could even throw a single punch, I grabbed a baseball bat left behind by one of those thugs and whacked my friend repeatedly until he left for that digital afterlife…and I saved that pretty pixelated princess.

After high-fiving my friend (he wasn't that upset that I clubbed him), we turned from the video game.

My phone started vibrating in my pocket and I began thinking about my afternoon meetings…wish we could stay 12 a little longer.

2020

January

I saved several hundred dollars over the holiday break by not reserving our airplane seats in advance. I thought this was a smart move. We had three flights, and my fantasy would be that since our flights were at weird times (one very late at night, one on Christmas Day, and one on New Year's Eve), the planes would be empty and it would just be the four of us and a bunch of flight attendants.

You can therefore imagine my shock when I checked in online for the first flight and the plane was completely full except for four middle seats at the back!

I broke it to my family gently that for the next six hours, we would not only be sitting separate from each other, we would also have the worst seats on the plane. In addition, we were Boarding Group 9—I didn't know there was a Boarding Group 9!

After being almost the last ones to board the plane, we each took our middle seats, our older daughter's seat right up against the bathroom in the last row.

Now, here is the part that is even more shocking than there being a Boarding Group 9—each of us had a great flight experience!

I now appreciate that middle seat more than ever!

Advantages include if you don't like talking with the person on the left you can talk with the person on your right (or ignore both people), you don't keep rubbing against that hard plastic shell of the window seat, and you don't get head-bumped by backpacks or elbow-bumped by the food and beverage carts as you would in the aisle seat.

We had two more flights during our trip, where as luck would have it, we all had middle seats. (Who wants to fly on Christmas Day? Apparently, a whole flight-load of people.)

We had pleasant experiences on all three flights.

The New Year has started off well—I have finally gotten over my fear of that dreaded middle seat! Happy 2020!

February

I look for opportunities to save money when I travel. For example, I recently flew to Phoenix and needed to rent a car at the airport. A few days before my trip, I searched online and found a good deal on a rental car. Even though I never heard of this company, let's call them "Ralph's Rental," their reviews weren't too bad, I could pick up the car at the airport, and they were half the price of Avis and Hertz. When I checked in at the rental car counter, I received a free car upgrade.

Two rental car tips for you.

First, when a rental car agent tries to sell you on a car upgrade, decline it because there's a good chance you will get that upgrade for free. This sales tactic is used when they don't have your car category available. They try to make extra money before eventually reluctantly handing you the keys to that upgrade for free. It has happened the last two times for me.

Second, the free upgrade was for a bright red sporty car with out-of-state plates. I could just picture getting pulled over for going 29 mph in a 25 zone for having a bright red car with California plates in Arizona. I switched to a family car with Arizona plates—now I can drive 80 in a 50 mph zone and no worries…remember, always in-state plates and choose minivans over sportscars.

Anyway, the whole experience was great renting through them, until I had to return the car at night. The issue was signage. Signs to the rental car center were large and well-lit. Once I arrived near the rental car return area, rental car return signs for Avis, Hertz, and other companies I have heard of before were also easy to spot.

I could not find Ralph's Rental car return signs, though!

I kept driving those typical airport circular roads, slowing down when I approached signs, to the point where even in friendly Arizona, cars behind me started beeping until, eventually, there was-a tiny sign directing me to Ralph's. It could have been a sign Ralph's daughter made at school with crayons.

A happy ending. I dropped off the car and made my flight. However, was it worth saving a few dollars for that extra excitement at the airport? Yes!

March

My wife and I tried to instill our love of hiking in our daughters ever since they were old enough to walk. When they were very young, we disguised hiking as a quest through the forest to spot mythical creatures like unicorns. When they got a little older, after a hike, we gave them ice cream. Now that they are both teenagers, we call it a "walk" instead of a "hike," there must always be a cell phone tower within eyesight, and we use only paved asphalt trails—and they still complain!

This past weekend, however, we took our younger daughter and one of her friends with us on a hike. According to our daughter, he likes to hike ('he' is the key word, by the way). The hike was more brutal than we anticipated—over five miles, mostly climbing up and down rocks.

Whenever I turned around to make sure her friend was still being a friend and not holding hands or anything, I heard laughter and bubbly conversation. Not one complaint from our daughter the entire hike! In fact, at the end of the hike, she said, "That was so much fun!"

We love going to estate sales and our daughter does not—however, we asked if her friend would like to come. As I am typing this, he is over our house and we are getting ready to go to two estate sales. I have a strong feeling that she will enjoy estate sales today!

April

Our dog Daisy barks when strangers approach our house, whines when she wants to go out, and chases away anything furry from a chipmunk to a bear—typical dog. However, unlike any other dog I know, she makes this guttural deep humming sound when she knows something good is about to happen. We hear this "something good is going to happen" sound when she knows she will get a treat, when she rolls over anticipating a belly rub, and when she knows it is time for a walk.

How can she be so certain that something good will happen?

Yet, she is always right. In times when media and politicians tell us "something bad is going to happen," it's comforting to hear that sound.

May

One of my dreams is to cruise the country in a motorhome. Looking for the silver lining with the virus, this dream may become closer to reality. I might have read too many Stephen King books, but I have this post-apocalypse Covid vision of driving around the country in an RV, visiting places like the Grand Canyon, and no one is there except for us.

But (and there's always a 'but'), motorhomes are big...years ago, I rented a motorhome and was too scared to drive it. I just left it parked in front of the house, and our one outing was going out for ice cream—I put only seven miles on a one-week RV rental!

Do you know how much it costs to rent that motor home per mile?!

Motorhomes also require constant maintenance...a car requires maintenance and a house requires maintenance, so multiply that maintenance together for a motorhome. Also, they take up lots of space and guzzle gas.

The trick I've discovered over years of looking for motorhomes is to keep it a dream. Look at the RV ads and maybe even make a phone call or two, plan the first road trip, or even call the insurance company to see how much it would cost to insure...but never actually buy one. This way, I can get all the excitement around potentially owning a motorhome without any stress.

Some dreams should remain dreams.

June

On Sunday, I took a big step closer to owning a motorhome. My family and I drove to see an RV for sale at a good price.

Pulling into the driveway, I realized why this huge old motorhome was so cheap. Only half of the rear bumper was attached, dents and cracks plagued the sides, and the front passenger door was missing a panel. I learned that a teenager used the motorhome to party with his friends. I opened the shower door and looked up and saw the sky—a panel was missing from the roof!

I started the engine, and the erratic humming sounded like the RV was pleading, "Please let me end it here and don't take me for a test drive."

A voice in my head louder than the complaining of the engine said, "You would have to be crazy to buy this." It didn't help that the family selling this motorhome had it parked in front of a scary-looking mansion they owned, which was America's first private insane asylum, the Craig House.

The most shocking part of this story, however, is that I came very close to buying this motorhome!

July

I flew cross-country a couple of weeks ago and was dreading the flight. I imagined a germ-fest full flight where everyone is coughing and…well you get the idea.

Instead, I boarded a plane that smelled like it was just dropped in lemon juice, no one sat in the middle seat, and everyone wore face masks. On most of my flights, you would hear a cough or sneeze every few minutes. I don't know if people were afraid to cough or sneeze, but I didn't hear a single sound the entire flight—not even someone clearing their throat! It's funny how most of the things we worry about turn out to be nothing to worry about after all.

Take face masks, for example. A month ago, I would worry about wearing a face mask. Now, I don't go anywhere without it.

I think part of the worry was the initial stigma of wearing a face mask. What a lousy name! We need a better name than 'face mask,' like 'face muffs' (ear muffs for the face). 'Muffs' is such a cute name.

Our younger daughter is already thinking about school fashion for the fall: "I need to have face masks that match my outfits each day."

And I think we can turn 'face masks' into a game called *Guess My Expression*. I played this game with our younger daughter. Make a completely silly face with your mask on, and see if they can guess your expression. It's amazing how easy it is to correctly guess—eyes give a lot away.

Try this too, next time you are in the supermarket wearing your face mask…um…face muffs, stick your tongue out at the person in line in front of you—very cool, they won't even know!

August

Let me tell you about the best Chinese restaurant in the world. And, by the way, I know Chinese food: I was complimented more than once in China for how I hold my chopsticks, two million travel miles have allowed me to eat at a lot of Chinese restaurants, and I once came in second place in a Chinese food eating competition (no joke).

The best Chinese restaurant is...drum roll please...the Golden Gate right here in New Jersey.

Look past the 1980s décor, laminated folding tables, and water-stained ceiling tiles, and you will enjoy exceptionally yummy food. But Mary is the reason why it ranks first. Mary owns the restaurant and she is an amazing hostess. She always sits us at our favorite table, and she has an incredible memory of our orders from previous visits.

"Mary, what was that great appetizer I had last time?" Note that *last time* was over five months ago.

"You had the cold sesame noodle with extra peanut sauce."

"That's right, and it was great. I'll take that again, plus do you remember what my entrée was?"

"You had the eggplant with garlic sauce."

"I'll get it again. Can you make it with the same level of spiciness as last time?"

And so on…

Mary's restaurant hasn't opened since March, and we fear it will not open again. We drive by or call every week to see if they are open.

The virus has taught me how much I take for granted, even with restaurants!

September

The summer is a great time to grow and pick up a new skill, and this summer, our dog has mastered the skill of escaping from our property.

Daisy's goal is to reach a retired couple's house, where she will receive a warm greeting, enjoy several hours of playtime with their two dogs, and receive way too many dog treats.

The escape skills she has developed this summer include pretending to be asleep, hiding behind outdoor furniture, and jumping over our fenced-in backyard.

For example, I let Daisy out and she "sleeps" on her outdoor bed until I turn away, then she scurries behind tables and chairs, stealthily making her way to the final challenge of jumping over our fence. She has escaped many times using this approach. Once in a while, we catch her and she sheepishly walks back to us with her head low—defeated until her next escape.

I wonder what she is thinking during her escapes. I imagine she enjoys the escaping process as much as the playtime and treats waiting for her if she succeeds. I can almost hear Mission Impossible music gently playing in her little dog head as she tries again and again to complete her quest.

October

"I am building a large house and need to dig a huge hole for a basement. Want the dirt for free that we excavate?"

"Sure," I replied to my contractor friend. How can I say "no" to free dirt? We could definitely use some dirt to level part of our property, and I began imagining a truck dropping off some dirt and then me throwing some grass seed over the dirt and just like "Jack and Beanstalk," the next day, we would have a beautiful lawn.

The contractor must have seen me daydreaming and added, "You can coordinate directly with my excavator to arrange payment for the bulldozer you'll need to level the dirt."

Looking back, this would have been a good time to say "no thanks" to the free dirt, but instead, I nodded my head and took the excavator's phone number. After paying for about a week of a bulldozer's time flattening over 30 truckloads of dirt around our property, I again imagined throwing down grass seeds and having a beautiful lawn the next day.

Chatting with the bulldozer driver during his lunch break, however, delivered the second blow. "You can't plant grass directly on dirt," he said, chuckling. "You'll need to bring in some top soil."

So we brought in 12 truckloads of top soil, and then the third blow came when we learned that we can't plant grass seed until we remove all of the large rocks and stones in the soil. We also identified many dead trees to take down before planting the grass seeds. This took a team of people three days to complete. Finally, the grass seed went down followed by a truckload of hay to cover the seeds.

I'm not a mathematician, but I did roughly sum up the cost of a dozen truckloads of topsoil, a week of bulldozer usage, 17 dead trees removed, three days of a team manually removing stones, and then finally planting grass seed and covering with hay—and I learned a very important lesson: there is no such thing as "free dirt"!

November

Around this time of year, three decades ago, I was in the throes of an intense graduate program—a two-year program condensed into 14 months containing advanced electrical engineering and computer science courses. I never took an engineering class in my life, and now, here I am, with 60

other graduate students who all live for engineering except for me—the only one completely lost during the lectures.

Survival in my classes, combined with living on my own in a strange new city, led to a very intense fall semester.

One cold evening in late November, while walking back from an electrical engineering class to my apartment, in deep thought about an upcoming exam, I heard a strange repeating sound. Crunch, crunch, crunch. I looked down, and the crunching sound was the noise of my sneakers on weathered brown leaves. It was nearing winter, and I completely missed the magic and leaf-changing beauty of fall! I was studying and stressing instead of enjoying the bright colors and crisp fall smells around me.

I never made that same mistake again. Hope you are enjoying the beautiful fall coolness and magic.

December

Our daughters, like many other high school students around the world, are taking their classes virtually. Sometimes, I'll open my office door and hear them learning math, science, or history. Sometimes, I'll hear them presenting or asking questions. Two weeks ago, our older daughter gave a presentation in Spanish. It was the first time I had heard her speak conversational Spanish. Muy bien! It seems like most classes work just as well in a virtual environment.

However, last week, I went into the kitchen for a glass of water and saw our younger daughter coloring a paper plate. "I'm making a steering wheel for driver's ed so we can practice driving," she said.

Learning how to drive virtually?

I almost dropped my glass. I can just picture a group of 16-year-old high school students sounding out engine and brake sounds as they turn their paper plates to merge on to virtual highways (Vroom!!).

I sure hope self-driving cars become widely available before our daughter's class hits the road!

2021

January

My wife and I love hiking. Our kids and dog, not so much.

Last week, after only a few minutes into a family hike, our younger daughter started asking when we're turning around. A few minutes later, we noticed our older daughter on her phone. "Not a good idea to hike while you're on your phone," I said. "I'm on Google Maps looking for shortcuts back to the car." Our daughters' complaints continued while we pulled our dog Daisy on her leash instead of her pulling us, like she normally does when we go for walks.

A short while down the trail, due to constant gripes from our daughters and the need to take turns carrying Daisy after she sat down in the dirt and refused to walk another step (and she is not a light dog), we decided to call it a day and end our hike early.

Yesterday, however, it was just my wife and I hiking. We went for a massively long and relaxing hike—no complaining and no furry companions to carry. About halfway into our hike, I commented how quiet it is with just the two of us.

My wife said nothing, and I let my mind wander into the near future when college and careers become priorities for our daughters, and it is always just my wife and I hiking.

Will I miss the kids complaining? Will I miss carrying the dog? Maybe we will squeeze in a short family hike tomorrow…

February

I like to think I'm getting younger over time, but three events in January proved the opposite.

First, another birthday, another year older.

Second, I cracked a molar. I always thought a tooth only breaks on something hard like a peach pit—I cracked a tooth on a donut! And I even dipped it in milk! What can be softer than a vegan chocolate donut dunked in almond milk? I won't go into the details of the root canal that followed—except that, even with all our amazing technology, how come a root canal is the same unpleasant experience it was when I was a teenager?

Third, I was riding a bike in a new area when I heard a siren behind me and a booming male voice over an intercom, "Sir, pull over." I glanced over my shoulder to see a police car with lights flashing. Now I was on a bike—not a motorcycle but a bicycle, and a girl's bike (different story though).

I must be the first person ever to get pulled over on a bicycle!

Two policemen exited the vehicle and walked towards me, each with a hand resting gently on their holsters. They explained that I did not stop at the stop sign and that the same rules for cars apply to bikes. Luckily, I didn't mention to them that I had biked through over a thousand stop signs over the years. Instead, I apologized and said it would not happen again.

Next, something strange happened: we had a really nice conversation. The two policemen, one male and one female, each probably less than half my age, reminded me of our daughters' friends, and I found myself asking about the area and themselves.

After learning where they went to high school, my phone rang, and I excused myself and rode away. No ticket, but I did stop at every stop sign on the way back to our house.

I don't know if I avoided getting a ticket because of our paternal conversation or because of the laughter both officers would have received after their colleagues learned they gave a ticket to a middle-aged bicyclist—maybe there are advantages to being 50-something.

March

Some winters in New Jersey are short and sweet—the mild fall weather extends into December, and the warm breezes of spring start early March.

This winter is not one of those.

In February, for example, after one exceptionally large snowstorm with strong wind gusts, it was actually hard to find one of our cars under the snow!

In the spirit of turning lemons into lemonade, last week I carried down my cross-country skis from the attic and forced myself to cross-country ski around our yard. It was way below freezing, and the yard was a sheet of ice, but I kept going. I made it around our yard one full time before losing control and wiping out on the ice, right behind our chicken coop.

As I tried to right myself, I realized wearing gloves would have been a good idea. I felt the icy wetness through my clothes and realized a jacket and ski pants would have been useful, too. Our two chickens, which I didn't hear a peep out of the whole time while skiing, suddenly began making a lot of noise, which sounded a little too much like laughter.

As I sat on the ice in my wet clothes, hands numb from the cold and scratched from the ice, hearing the chickens laugh at me, I started visualizing a warm comfortable winter in Florida or Arizona…maybe next year.

April

Some people have a green thumb with vegetation thriving in their presence. I have the opposite of a green thumb. In fact, a great investment strategy would be to take out life insurance policies on all the plants trusted to my care over the years. I even somehow managed to kill a cactus—and in less than a month! Aren't cactus' supposed to live hundreds of years?

A couple of weeks ago, my wife bought me a hyacinth plant. Hyacinths are beautiful plants with strong sweet spring smells. I told myself I would do whatever it takes to make this plant live a long time. I kept it on my desk under a light, watered it several times a day, and talked to it occasionally (very good conversations, by the way).

Yet even with all this care, within a week, the plant started looking like all the other plants after I take care of them for a week. I doubled my efforts—more light, more water, more talking, yet still, the hyacinth continued to brown and wither. As a last resort, I propped it up using an old dog collar and thermos (don't even ask where this idea came from).

Anyway, a few days ago, I went into my office looking for my plant. It was gone. My wife confirmed that it had joined all of the other plants in plant heaven that I have tried to take care of over the years.

I think next year, I will buy a hyacinth candle and skip the plant.

May

Being a data person, I live on spreadsheets. Even for life-changing decisions, rows become decision factors, columns become decisions, and I choose the highest sum of the weighted scores from each decision/decision factor cell—logical, unemotional, consistent.

A few weeks ago, our older daughter had narrowed down which university to attend to two. Both have good programs, are located in beautiful areas, and are equally far away from home. She flew with my wife to visit the one in Arizona, and a week later, she went with me to the one in Colorado.

Even as we sat at the gate in the Denver Airport waiting for our return flight early Saturday morning, she had not yet decided.

So, I confidently powered on my laptop, and together, we created one of my never-fail weighted score spreadsheets and…it didn't work for her.

Discouraged, I went to find a water fountain to fill up our water bottles. It took about 15 minutes to find a water fountain that was not wearing a garbage bag (definitely a Covid thing), and when I returned, she seemed more relaxed and told me that her friends will decide for her.

Now, I know some of her friends, and so, while trying to hold in a primal scream that would definitely close the airport for hours, she said she created a 30-question survey, asked her friends to complete it, and already received 16 responses.

We still had a few minutes before boarding, so I asked to take the survey. The questions were short but covered the decision factors:

"Desert or Mountain?"

"Skateboard or Sail?"

"Bad food or bad water?"

I was amazed at the speed that she created and distributed the survey, yet even more amazed that most of her friends responded in minutes on an early Saturday morning. It was like one collective teenage brain.

By the time we landed in Newark, the rest of her friends had responded, and she tallied the scores and made her decision.

The desert it is!

June

Do you remember some of those scary dreams we had as kids, like monsters in the closet, wearing your pajamas to school, and creepy clowns? Luckily we forget them soon afterward, and if we did remember them today, they would probably make us laugh (except for those clowns).

I did have one scary dream when I was about eight that resurfaced recently. My family and I were driving through a desert when my dad stopped the car and I got out. Then they drove away as I played with my toys in the sand—that was the dream!

Not as scary as clowns, but I remember waking up feeling sad and uncomfortable after being uprooted to this foreign sandy terrain.

Fast forward to today. Our older daughter is going to college in Arizona, and we've decided to move and follow her. We are leaving our roots in New York and New Jersey and moving to the desert…Arizona.

When I told my mom we were moving, those same being-far-away-from-home emotions I had in that dream bounced right back as fresh as they felt 45 years ago.

I wonder if it is wise to follow your dreams, even the scary ones…we will find out.

July

I am convinced our 16-year-old landed her dream job this summer at the Jersey Shore. She is a beach badge checker. Four days a week, she bikes a mile to the beach, sets up a chair and umbrella, and lounges for six hours while checking people's beach badges. A cool breeze almost always blows off the ocean, even on hot summer days. I would pay to do this job!

Last week, I suggested that she read while sitting under her umbrella, and to my surprise, she asked me for a book. So I loaned her a large hard-covered book that explains how the mind works. (By the way, "The Inner Game of Tennis" is a great read, even if you are not a tennis player.)

Yesterday, I bike rode with her, and as we were setting up her umbrella, I asked about the book. It was quiet for a moment, and then she said that she wasn't really *reading* the book—she keeps it propped up in front of her while on her phone. "Looks better that way," she said.

I shook my head and began thinking of the wonderful opportunities that await a book publisher who can offer books on Instagram or TikTok.

August

Last week, we drove from New Jersey to Arizona. It's always wise to plan for the unexpected with long road trips. Pack plenty of water and snacks (for me, this means lots of chocolate!), some band-aids, and a good audiobook. Change the oil, check the tire pressure, and top off the windshield wiper fluid. And then, expect a Zen-filled relaxing car ride…until your air conditioner stops working somewhere in the middle of Ohio.

I thought New Jersey had warm summers. Ohio, Indiana, Missouri, Oklahoma—it kept getting hotter and hotter! We kept telling ourselves that the next state would be cooler. My phone actually gave up and overheated just outside of St. Louis! I panicked for a moment, realizing I could no longer follow Google Maps on my phone, and then remembered I still had another 1,400 miles to go on this particular highway!

It seemed to keep getting warmer in the car, even with the windows rolled down. It was 98 degrees with high humidity at 7 pm in Clinton, Oklahoma, when we finally decided to call it a day and check in to a hotel.

We took our luggage and some snacks up to the room. I try to believe that every cloud has a silver lining, and sure enough, while sifting through our snack bag, I noticed that the summer heat had replaced the chocolate bars in my plastic container with a steaming chocolate sludge.

I grabbed a plastic spoon, sat on the hotel bed in our air-conditioned room, and enjoyed every sip of that hot liquid chocolate—it was the best dessert I ever had!

I now realize that every cloud has a *chocolate* lining!

September

The statistic that bugs outnumber people 200 million to one didn't faze me until moving to Arizona.

Two weeks ago, in preparation for a rainstorm, I unclogged several drains filled with metal mesh—why would there be metal mesh in our drains?

I found out why last Monday, when a tarantula walked through one of the now unclogged drains. It was so big that as it crawled around our dog's water bowl, I kept picturing the spider using the water bowl as a hot tub. It moved slowly, deliberately, and eventually, opened our gate and left (or squeezed under the gate, I wasn't sure).

On Tuesday, we were watching a movie, and our younger daughter asked if that was a spider on the ceiling. I glanced up and first thought it was a bat (which would have been less scary). As an impulse, I hurried to our garage to retrieve a bug gun I bought while in New Jersey—this gun uses air to safely suck in the bug, and then you can release it outside.

I loaded the gun and pointed it at this spider. My hands trembled as I realized, too late, that I should have left this useless gun in New Jersey where bugs are normal-sized, and instead invested in a harpoon.

On Wednesday, while getting ready for bed, I turned on the light in the bedroom, and this large leggy thing rushed at me. At first, I thought it was a centipede—but then, I realized it was a scorpion! It took a plastic container, a magazine, and 30 minutes of stressful scorpion hunting to eventually contain the scorpion and identify its marks as a bark scorpion (not one of the friendly scorpions).

Three days in a row of meeting scary critters—hoping we met all of the scary ones in Arizona.

October

I didn't realize how much I missed in-person gatherings until last week. I attended the local photography club's presentation on getting the big picture during photo shoots. This was the first in-person meeting I attended in 18 months, and it felt fantastic to be in the same physical room with other people!

Right when the presenter approached the podium, however, the projector sizzled and turned off. Oh, the unpredictability of live events…what excitement! Before I knew what was happening, I found myself on the stage playing with the projector. In a couple of minutes, the projector came back to life. As I stood up from behind the projector table, people applauded.

Real, live applause—what a rush!

November

Not too long ago, if you needed an electrician, they would be there the next day. No more! Where did everybody go?

Two weeks ago, I needed an electrician, and the only one who responded said that he is scheduling for one-month out and has ten people on his waiting list! So, with the help of YouTube, I completed the electrical project myself. (And only got electrocuted once.)

We could not even find someone to teach our younger daughter how to drive. So I decided to teach her. After several driving lessons, I learned that she does not respond well to verbal feedback. For example, if I tell her she is drifting in her lane too much to the right, she replies with "Stop judging me!" or "You are ruining my concentration!" So, I started using hand signals, such as pointing my hand left to move the car more left. This technique works well.

Except for yesterday. My wife was driving and I instinctively pointed my hand left since she was too close to the car next to us. My wife did not respond as well as my daughter does to the hand signals.

When self-driving cars become widely available, I will be first in line!

December

Have you ever tried removing wallpaper?

After watching a few YouTube videos, I decided to remove the 1980s-era wallpaper in our kitchen. I asked Alexa to play some Spa music, and armed with a spray bottle and spackle knife, I started scraping away.

Removing the first layer of wallpaper was a complete Zen experience. Pulling off large strips of wallpaper as Enya played in the background was like a day at a spa. Next, I started working on the second layer of wallpaper (the layer with the glue backing), and quickly, my experience turned from a day at the spa to a day at the dentist.

I worked viciously on an area the size of a shoe for hours, with the spa music hard to hear over the sounds of my spackle knife removing shards of drywall, leaving a Swiss cheese-looking finish to my work.

Although I am less than halfway done removing the paper, I have already gained a valuable insight from this painful experience—and that is how beautiful paneling would look in our kitchen.

2022

January

I love cruising. It's magical to wake up in the morning, look outside, and see a new port to explore.

We went on a seven-night cruise two weeks ago to the Mexican Riviera, leaving from San Diego. After the stress of finding a parking space for our oversized van in San Diego for less than $75 a day and proving our negative Covid tests before boarding, we ran to be the first to board the ship in anticipation of the fun that lay ahead.

The first four days were fantastic—the ship was only at half occupancy, the food delicious, and the entertainment excellent. Cabo San Lucas, our first port, was beautiful. In Mazatlán, our second port, we zip-lined from tree to tree and sampled local Tequila (note, not at the same time). However, after waiting over two hours to disembark at our third port, Puerto Vallarta, the captain announced that since 24 crew members have Covid, no one is allowed off, and we are returning to San Diego.

We didn't know any crew members had Covid—yikes!

During the next three days at sea, we reached our quota in organized trivia challenge games, walks around the veranda, and buffets (I impressed myself after eating four desserts after a large dinner on Day 6). We had to get off this ship, even if it meant swimming back to San Diego.

We were the first ones both on and off the ship.

Would we cruise again? Definitely! Maybe we'll wait a bit, though, until this Pandemic is history.

February

It was a big move from New Jersey to Arizona, but so far so good. My wife has her pickleball networks and our younger daughter has decent high school friends and works in a clothing store after school. I am most impressed, however, with how our dog Daisy has found her groove.

Daisy growls at the UPS delivery guy even louder than she did in New Jersey. She howls at the javelina and coyotes with more spirit than she did with deer and foxes in New Jersey. She barks at us if we forget to feed her or take her for a walk, with a greater sense of entitlement than she had in New Jersey.

However, she has also expanded her vocal range. She has developed a new sound, half whine and half yelp, to call over our neighbors to deliver her daily treats. I have watched more than once in horror from the kitchen window, as our neighbors, who are way into their eighties, take turns risking their lives climbing over rocks and skirting between razor-sharp bushes as they navigate from their property to ours in response to Daisy's cry for a dog biscuit.

She has trained them well!

March

From her elementary school years through most of high school, we always had to squint to find our older daughter in class pictures.

"Found her in that corner again!"

"Why is she hiding behind that tall kid?"

"Isn't that her shoulder between those two?"

Towards the end of high school, however, either my eyesight was getting better or it was becoming easier to spot her in a class picture. She would appear more towards the middle of the picture, smiling right at the camera.

Now that she is in college, whenever I see a picture of her with her friends or with her sailing club, even on my small phone screen or without wearing my glasses, I can find her right away. She is always right in the middle with her arms wrapped around the shoulders of the people on either side, wearing bright clothes and a confident big smile.

We can measure personal growth in terms of knowledge, accomplishments, or endurance…with our older daughter, however, photograph placement is a key performance indicator!

April

Our "to do" list leading up to vacation includes adjusting the thermostat, packing our suitcases (with way much more stuff than we will ever need), and dropping off our dog Daisy at a pet sitter.

We used to feel a little guilty leaving Daisy behind, but since her current pet sitter provides her with so much entertainment and enrichment, we think Daisy would like us to stay on our vacation forever.

After dropping her off two weeks ago, her pet sitter began sending us a constant stream of pictures and videos. Daisy going down the slide at the playground, Daisy munching on McDonald's chicken nuggets, Daisy taking long walks…even Daisy stretched out on their couch! (We don't let her on our furniture.)

The day before we picked her up, we received a video of her creating a watercolor—a painting where she used her paws to create a flower garden!

As I admire her painting prominently displayed in our kitchen, I wonder if we kept Daisy there for another week, would she come back knowing how to play tennis and practice yoga?

May

How can we measure the progress of a home renovation project beyond just time and money?

Take pain, for example. Wouldn't it be interesting to know that a home renovation project costs $200,000, took ten months, and scored a 72.5 in pain? I think our current home renovation project would score very high in all three of these categories, especially pain.

Fond recent memories include forgetting to turn off the circuit breaker and brushing the live black wire against a metal junction box while balancing on 12-foot metal scaffolding—what fireworks! And right in our living room!

Stepping on nails that always seem to find the thinnest part of my shoes' soles. Wood splinters, metal splinters, glass splinters—even vinyl flooring splinters! Pain from repetitive tasks like lifting 60 sheets of drywall, prying off 500 feet of molding, pulling out 5,000 carpet staples, running 200 feet of electrical wire, carrying four tons of garbage to a dumpster, replacing 90 outlets and switches, and much more.

A very high pain surcharge occurred last week. While trying to push the wires back into a recessed lighting fixture in our kitchen ceiling, my ladder slipped out from under me and I actually "rode" it down 14 feet, landing squarely on the floor while still gripping the ladder! As the emergency room doctor brilliantly summarized, "Patient fell with ladder, and on ladder."

As I am typing this sentence, calculating the pain from my sprained wrist, several broken toes, multiple bruises, and a completely crushed iPhone 12 Pro (which hurt the most), I wonder what our pain score would be in this project…

June

Have you ever wanted to run a marathon? Having the endurance and willpower to go mile after mile, mind over body, until you reach the finish line? My family and I ran our first marathon two weeks ago. We drove nonstop from Arizona to New Jersey.

We weren't running, we were driving, but we did cover about one hundred times the length of the typical marathon.

We didn't eat protein gels and other healthy foods, but we did polish off two grocery bags of chips and cookies. We didn't drink water or Gatorade, we drank coffee and soda. We didn't get the adrenaline rush of running past each mile marker, but we did get the adrenaline rush of seeing the incredibly high gas bill every few hours when we stopped to refuel.

I drove both red-eye shifts. When I used to fly a lot, I always opted for the red-eye. I always liked the otherworldly feeling of being awake when the rest of the world sleeps. I got the same feeling while driving through the night. Just me and a bunch of truckers cruising the highways, trying to reach the next state before dawn.

I am already training for our next family marathon when we drive back to Arizona in August.

July

We recently attended our first family gathering since Covid. We drove from New Jersey to New York for the party, and it actually took less time to drive through the entire state of Oklahoma than it did to travel roundtrip through the Bronx and Queens. If you ever need to explain the concept of traffic to somebody, recommend a drive through the Bronx (at any time of day).

Anyway, the party was fantastic. I haven't seen most of our relatives for over two years, and it was amazing how people have changed since Covid, both inside and out. My clean-cut cousin now has a ponytail, an older relative who always gave suffocating hugs told us not to get close, and everyone seemed to be talking about politics, which was a topic we always avoided in the past.

I know I changed too. I found myself wanting to talk to my relatives. In the past, I would rather hide in the basement playing ping pong or deep in the yard playing Frisbee over lots of chit-chat. Now, I sat and talked.

As I was thinking about these observations while sitting in the Bronx traffic during the long drive back to New Jersey, our younger daughter interrupted my thoughts. "Tomorrow's Father's Day, you know."

Where has time gone? I can't believe Father's Day is here. I spent the next five minutes in the car explaining to my family how I would like Father's Day to go, starting with chocolate chip pancakes for breakfast.

Sure enough, Father's Day was amazing. While working through my second plate of chocolate chip pancakes, I heard a beep from my wife's phone, and she read the incoming text with shock. "Father's Day is next Sunday, not today!"

We got the date wrong. I'm not complaining.

How cool is that to get two Father's Day celebrations!

August

Since last week was our last full week at the Jersey Shore before driving back home to Arizona, we needed to squeeze in as many New Jersey sunsets as possible before leaving the state. (Yes, there are beautiful Jersey sunsets!)

Late in the week, while walking pass a tennis court after watching the sunset, our younger daughter noticed something bright in a garbage can by the tennis court gate. She stuck her arm in the garbage can and pulled out a dress—just like a magician pulling a rabbit out of a hat! We were all shocked.

My wife and I were extra shocked because she does not like getting anywhere near garbage—try asking her to take the garbage out!

She washed the dress when we got home, and now she has a new dress. I don't know the strange situation that led to an expensive dress (still with its tags) hiding in a garbage can, but the outcome was euphoric.

Have you ever had an unexplainable and bizarre positive event?

I could not think of my own, but a few years ago, during a walk, our dog, Daisy, poked her head into a bush and pulled out a half-eaten ham and cheese sandwich! It was like magic!

In the backdrop of a crazy world, it's nice to experience magic.

September

It was a light drizzle, and my dog, Daisy, and I went for a walk. When we reached the distance furthest away from our house, the drizzle turned into a downpour. The street turned into a small river, with toe-high waves cresting over my sandals and covering Daisy's paws.

This is monsoon season—why didn't I bring an umbrella?

In less than a minute, I felt like I had just jumped into a pool. I looked down at Daisy, who hates getting wet, still walking at her usual pace, trudging along towards home as rain pelts her from all sides.

As I continued to get soaked, I tried to think positive thoughts to the sounds of my sandals squishing with my steps. "Rain is good. We need rain. I needed to cool off anyway. I was thinking about getting new sandals."

I then glanced up for a second to see if the sky was getting lighter, and saw the most brilliant rainbow. Bright blues and reds and purples, and completely unobstructed, so I could almost see the beginning and end. Amazing! Then I looked down at Daisy, still trudging along in the rain, who I am guessing cannot see this beautiful rainbow.

What is her rainbow?

When we got home, I gave her two long towel rubs and a treat.

October

I grew up in Queens, just a few miles from Manhattan, and always imagined camping one day—breathing fresh air, hiking during the day, and seeing endless stars at night. A few weeks ago, I experienced camping for the first time.

Our local camera club organized a photo shoot at Hunt's Mesa, a remote part of Monument Valley in Utah. It was just one night, and our Navajo tour guides drove us four hours in vintage Chevy Suburbans for the steep 2,000-foot ascent to the top of the mesa.

Along the way, one car overheated and another car sank deep into the sand. My car reached the top, even with a missing door on my side and a dangling front bumper. (These Suburbans should have moved on to their next life after several hundred thousand miles of Uber driving—instead, they will spend the rest of their days huffing and puffing up a trail that would deter even advanced hikers.)

We finally made it to the top way after nightfall. I pitched my tent in complete darkness and had the feeling (which I confirmed in the morning) that it looked less like a tent and more like a burlap sack tossed over a cactus.

4 am to 7 am were my favorite three hours of the trip. I finally dozed off, successfully blocking out the snoring and other human sounds from the surrounding tents. A very slight breeze shook my tent enough to wake me. A mystic would have sensed ancient Native American spirits playing tag around our tents.

I quietly dressed in complete darkness, walked beyond our tents to a clearing, and looked up.

I have never seen so many stars! I stared up at the millions of stars until my neck hurt, and then sat on a rock overlooking all of Monument Valley to watch the sunrise.

I could have done without the other 30 hours or so of my camping experience.

Would I go camping again? It depends on how you define "camping." If camping includes staying overnight at a Hilton, count me in!

November

Halloween is one of my favorite holidays. I spend hours scouring thrift shops and yard sales every year, searching for festive or spooky shirts, pants, hats, and other accessories that magically mesh for that perfect costume. My annual budget for costumes is $10—even with inflation!

After several hours of diligent hunting this year, I put together enough bright pieces of clothing to go as a hot air balloon, and it only costs $5.50!

However, I've noticed a trend over the last few years. As I search my town for Halloween outfits, my family searches my wardrobe for their costumes.

Over the last few Halloweens, they have repurposed many of my everyday outfits as their costumes. I started questioning my fashion sense two years ago when my older daughter and her friends asked if they could borrow a bunch of my bright flowery shirts to use as a Halloween Hawaiian theme. I can find our younger daughter in my closet whenever a 1980s event comes up at school (I think she still has my green Adidas track outfit I wore in high school).

This year, my wife was frantically looking for a costume for a Halloween pickleball party, and was relieved to find a shirt and hat of mine to wear. "I'm going to go as a tourist," she said, holding a shirt (that I wore last week) in one hand and one of my hiking hats in her other hand.

I've done some serious soul-searching this Halloween, and I think I'll wear one of my everyday outfits next year and put my $10 costume budget to better use.

Hope you had a fun and sweet Halloween!

December

When I was a senior in high school, I signed up for public speaking. Since I went to a rough New York City public school where any public speaking would probably get you chased down a stairway, only three of us "nerds" signed up. So, school administration canceled the class and moved us into a mime class.

Isn't mime the opposite of public speaking? Anyway, I had a knack for mime but, like most of my classes in high school, doubted it would ever come in handy.

Time passed like it always does, and our younger daughter, then about seven, complained about monsters in her closet and behind her bedroom door. We tried many ways to keep the monsters at bay, but what finally worked was me building a wall (using my mime skills) followed by reciting the phrase, "You can go out, we can come in, and nothing bad can come in." Those monsters were no match for my mime skills, and eventually, they moved on…until recently.

Kids mature into young adults, and monsters mature from big furry things into teenage worries.

Our younger daughter described some of her "monsters" to us last week. Pretty scary. But again, no match for my mime skills. I built a wall around her bed and impressed myself by still being able to recite the incantation a decade later, "You can go out, we can come in, and nothing bad can come in."

She took a deep breath, smiled, and went to bed.

2023

January

I have always wanted to hike to the summit of Capital Butte, known as the Mount Everest of Sedona. It shadows all surrounding peaks and intimidates all hikers (including me).

A couple of weeks ago, a professional mountain climber volunteered to take a small group to the summit, including my wife and me. It was a very difficult hike and rock scramble. There were several moments of huffing and puffing where I questioned my sanity, including one section where we needed to dig our fingers into a small notch in the rock and shift our weight, letting momentum take us around a cliff—yikes!

After hours of uphill hiking and rock climbing, we finally reached the top. We congratulated ourselves and sat together at the peak of Capital Butte, munching on sandwiches and snacks.

As we bragged about past and planned hiking conquests, a large black bird flew towards us. I thought the raven would just fly by us, but instead, it swooped down towards us and then glided effortlessly out over the valley, thousands of feet above the rocks and cactuses, and started rolling through the air—like a dog rolling on carpeting!

We oohed and ahhed as the bird executed its loops and barrel rolls. It performed this aerial circus act for several minutes before flying back into the distance.

Why this show? We could see no other ravens, so it was not trying to impress. Was it for pure fun? Or…was it mocking us? "Keep thinking you can conquer nature one hike at a time. But no matter how large your ambitions, you'll never be able to do even a single spin through the clouds." We quietly finished our lunch and began our descent.

February

I often quickly glance into the bathroom mirror while brushing my teeth or shaving, but sometimes I linger longer on my reflection while a strange guy in his mid-50s stares back at me. This can't be me! Who is this guy? His hair is thinning (ok, maybe disappearing), and what hair remains is mostly gray.

Where did that 25-year-old go?

This past week, in an effort to erase a few decades, I decided to color my hair. I bought this tube with a plastic comb, and our younger daughter smeared the goo in my hair with the same gusto as when painting a fine work of art.

The end result? I still can't find that 25-year-old, but that guy looking back at me in the mirror now looks in his early 50s instead of his mid-50s.

What to work on next? Maybe a time machine…

March

Although Arizona is landlocked, Arizona State University has a sailing team and our older daughter is captain this year. Her passion for sailing led the club to participate in many boat races ("regattas") along the California coast. It's a long drive from Phoenix to the West Coast, and therefore, when she announced that her team would be entering the San Luis

Obispo (abbreviated as SLO and pronounced "slow") regatta, I volunteered to be the driver.

I have always wanted to see one of her regattas, and we have a large van nicknamed "The Beast" that can comfortably fit the group going to this race. Our daughter mulled over my offer, and when I agreed to throw in free gas (gas is not cheap in California) and not talk about data modeling or listen to or participate in any conversations I should not listen to or participate in, she agreed.

I was excited and started packing shorts, T-shirts, and sandals, anticipating a sunny California weekend getaway. I pictured myself stretched out on a lounge chair on a warm beach, watching the sailboats in the distance.

Halfway to SLO, we hit a blizzard, adding five hours to the drive. I never knew Southern California gets snow! My shorts and sandals offered no protection from the freezing temperatures that first morning of the regatta. Trying to be the cool dad, I convinced the regatta's Safety Team while shivering and through chattering teeth of my boating expertise, and they assigned me to a patrol boat. This way, I can take pictures of our daughter and her team.

Within five minutes after leaving the shore, I heard the captain of my boat say, "Here it comes."

Before I could ask what is coming, hail pelted us from every direction. Our boat was quickly filling up with large pieces of ice, and I could barely hear the captain over the howling wind and the sound of ice smashing into fiberglass say, "Take pictures. This is rare!" I couldn't feel my hands and so couldn't take pictures. During the next few hours on the boat, the weather varied from hail to rain to hail, and when I finally got off the boat, it felt like I had swam in the icy bay.

The weather during the rest of the weekend wasn't much better, yet the kids from Arizona State and about 15 other schools had a complete blast.

When we settled into the Beast Sunday afternoon, our daughter and her teammates all agreed they loved the weekend's races, despite the weather.

During the long drive through the night, I thought about staying young. Maybe it has less to do with dying my hair from grey to brown, and more to do with laughing with friends on a tiny sailboat in the middle of a hailstorm.

April

After honeymooning in Hawaii, I promised my wife we would return for our 10th anniversary. And so, we returned for the 17th anniversary of our 10th anniversary.

In preparing for our 27th-anniversary adventure, I stopped by a local thrift shop and bought a book on Hawaii. Why spend $20 for a new travel book when you can have a

"Completely Revised" 1982 edition of Hidden Hawaii for just a dollar? Besides, I quickly browsed the line drawing map of the Hawaiian islands on the inside cover, and as far as I knew, all of these islands are still there today. How much can change in 40 years?

I was pretty proud of my purchase until I was planning a bike rental on the Big Island. The book recommended United Rent All to rent bikes. Call 935-2974. No web address, email address, or even area code! I told myself that there was a good chance United Rent All had gone out of business sometime over the last forty years anyway, so I just Googled bike rentals instead. Not a big deal.

On Maui, however, we planned on visiting a very popular beach. Since Covid, you have to make reservations way in advance. Same with watching the Haleakala Sunrise. In addition to not mentioning anything about making reservations, the book's many other omissions made me very aware of the high price of a cheap travel guide.

The book did have a good section on learning the local language, and I realized I am a lolo okole for buying that $1 travel guide!

May

I always thought "graceful aging" was an oxymoron, like "jumbo shrimp," "working vacation," and "virtual reality."

Our dog Daisy, however, is aging with style. We adopted her from the shelter nine years ago when she was a year old. So she's approaching retirement in human years. She has not changed in some ways. She still barks like crazy at the UPS guy, gives us at least a one-hour warning in the form of constant whining as dinner time approaches, and would easily choose one real hamburger over a full refrigerator of our vegan cuisine.

However, she has mellowed over the years. We noticed that she has become more tolerant of other dogs, takes a few extra naps each day, and prefers shorter walks.

Last week, we took her on one of our favorite hikes, which she has done several times. Instead of pulling most of the hike and wanting to lead the way, Daisy preferred walking slowly and taking many breaks. She wanted us to think she was admiring the flowers during our rare super bloom season, but I know she was catching her breath and preserving her energy for the full hike.

The hike took much longer than usual, but Daisy made it the whole way with still enough energy to keep that tail wagging.

Wagging your tail no matter how old you get, now that's "graceful aging."

June

Last week, we drove 40 hours straight from Sedona, Arizona, to the Jersey Shore. I drove through the first night and got us into New Mexico. My wife got us through Texas, our older daughter through Oklahoma, and our younger daughter took us deep into Missouri. After a few hours of driving, our younger daughter exited the highway for gas and lunch. She went right instead of staying straight and, frustrated, stopped the car in the middle of the busy road and said, "What do I do?"

She is a good driver. After all, she drove a large van filled with stuff and us for a few hundred miles. You can teach someone how to drive, but how do you teach someone not to fluster?

Maybe it comes with experience. Maybe I should buy her a Douglas Adams "Don't Panic" sticker. Or maybe we just need more Zen. Our town of Sedona is full of Zen. Sedona has more yoga, crystal, and aura shops than anywhere else.

A few weeks ago in Sedona, while at a traffic light, I noticed the car's license plate in front: JOYFU1. I then looked at the car's license plate in the middle lane: PEACEBE. Within minutes, I saw another license plate: ENLIGTN. As a teenager in New York, my license plate was CRPEDIEM. Maybe we have finally found our town.

The closer we got to New Jersey, the more of a culture shock. We stopped for gas at a crowded gas station in Pennsylvania, and somebody actually beeped at me. Beeped at me! Nobody beeps in Sedona. I remember something on a Pennsylvania license plate about having a friend in Pennsylvania. This guy was definitely not my friend.

The Jersey Shore is very different from Sedona, and it always takes a few days to adjust. Not many yoga or crystal places here. In fact, many days, I wake up and feel as if cast as a minor character in The Sopranos. We have a neighbor who will not wear a shirt from Memorial Day to Labor Day, and another neighbor about half my age who drives a Ferrari and is in the "landscaping business." It's noisy and crowded—there are fireworks on Wednesdays, weekend parties, blasting radios from muscle cars, and racing engines from souped-up speedboats.

During our ride through Arizona, New Mexico, Texas, Oklahoma, Missouri, Illinois, Indiana, Ohio, West Virginia, Pennsylvania, and finally into New Jersey, we must have driven right past so many interesting towns, each with their own unique culture. Wouldn't it be cool to have the time to immerse yourself into each town's culture?

Instead, I will be content with the start and end points, Sedona's Zen and the Jersey Shore's Electricity.

July

How do you define a "good" dog? Obedient? Submissive? Has restraint? Trustworthy?

Our dog Daisy was none of these. She was not obedient. "Daisy, stop pulling so hard." "Daisy, stop barking at our neighbor." "Daisy, stop doing that to her leg."

She was the opposite of submissive. She went after a bear in our yard, bit one of our neighbor's friends (whose parents are attorneys), and attacked a woman at a craft show. I know when Daisy saw her reflection in a puddle, it was of a massive Doberman instead of a little Beagle and Jack Russell mix.

Daisy had no restraint. She once made a hole in our deck clawing for a piece of food.

Trustworthy? Before we adopted her, she was a street dog and loved to run away. Even under watchful eyes, she would move to a cushion and pretend to be asleep. Then work her way under a picnic table and, finally, make her escape from our property.

She has escaped from our yard over a thousand times over the last ten years, but yesterday, it did not end well.

In less than two hours, I went from rubbing her belly on my lap to burying her in our yard. When a person dies, logistics ensures a minimal grieving period. But when a pet dies, you grab a shovel from the garage, bury them in the yard, drop their toys off at an animal shelter, and it's done.

Quiet here now. No pitter-patter of paw nails on the floor. No barking when the doorbell rings and someone drops off condolence flowers.

She was a good dog, though. She would run to us in the mornings, jumping on us with kisses. She would cry with excitement and run in circles when we returned after leaving her alone for hours. She put up with a 40-hour cross-country drive without air conditioning in the middle of July.

We may have to expand our definition of a "good" dog.

August

I love morning runs on the beach at the Jersey Shore. Shoes sinking slightly in the sand, deep breaths of cool salty ocean air, and the only sounds are my thoughts mixed with ocean waves.

I don't see many people early in the morning, but last week, I ran by a dad and two young boys as they made their way onto the beach. The dad pulled a blue wonder wheeler filled with umbrellas, towels, and toys with one hand, and held his phone to his ear with his other hand. I could hear parts of a business conversation, slightly out of breath with the strain of pulling the wagon wheels over sand.

The two boys behind him, hands filled with toys, ran onto the sand and plopped down, still a long walk from the ocean. One of the boys blurted out with excitement the most important command in our language: "Let's play!"

I ran past them as I heard these words, and glanced in their direction as they set up their plastic castles and action figures in the sand. "Let's play."

When I was little, I am sure I said this phrase often. This sentence got a little longer in the work-intensive decades of my twenties to forties: "Let's try to make time for play." Now, in my fifties, this sentence has several variations, but it is even longer: "Let's try to make time for play, as long as I don't get hurt or feel sore the next day."

I sometimes wonder when play became part of a schedule or worry.

On Friday, in the middle of prioritizing my "to do" list for the day, which included integrating several data models, redesigning our publishing website, editing a book, and evaluating speaking proposals for our conference, our younger daughter walked in and asked if I wanted to go for a bike ride to the Park Bakery for crumb cake.

My work thoughts were replaced with the realization that this is her only day of the week off from her summer job, and she leaves us to start college in a few weeks.

"Yes, definitely," I said without a second thought.

Let's play.

September

We recently drove cross-country from New Jersey back to Arizona. I pack our van (nicknamed the "Beast") considering accessibility (bags containing chocolate near me), fragility (avoid putting anything on top of our older daughter's cactus collection—cacti do not stack well), and supportability (big heavy boxes on the bottom and our younger daughter's 20 white trash bags of clothing on top, resembling a mountain's snow cap).

After completing this life-sized game of Tetris, my wife vacuums the car while I clean the windows. I imagine completing the 40-hour 2,400-mile drive without drama and the Beast being in the same state as when we started the trip. Just a dream, though.

The back air conditioner stopped working early in the trip, so we purchased a portable air conditioner for our younger daughter and several gallons of water for her to keep refilling the unit.

Somewhere in rural Pennsylvania, our older daughter decided to exit the Pennsylvania Turnpike to try a "shortcut" through farm country. She insisted on maintaining the same speeds as the Turnpike, taking sharp country road turns at nearly 80 miles an hour.

During one sharp turn, I heard a scream from our younger daughter as the gallon of water in the air conditioner erupted, spewing water everywhere in the cabin. The next hairpin caused an avalanche of her clothing bags, one bag landing inches from the prized cactus collection.

By early morning the next day, popcorn pieces and fast food wrappers littered the floor, the once sparkling clean windshield transformed into an abstract work of squashed bug art, and anywhere we weren't sitting contained the avalanche remains of open bags and boxes.

By the time we reached Missouri, accessibility, fragility, and supportability were replaced with coexistability, survivability, and immovability.

And this was only halfway to Arizona!

October

My wife and I just returned from an Alaskan cruise—our first trip without the kids now that both are in college. In the past, our family cruises were on large ships with lots of activities for families.

This was our first time cruising on a small ship aimed at the 55 and over crowd, and we took every opportunity to engage with other passengers. We ate our meals at shared tables, talked to people in front of us while waiting in lines, and chatted with people by the pool. I enjoyed the conversations, even if they were not about data. For example, I enjoyed talking with Brian, a retired ER doctor from Calgary, for over an hour about his antler collection. I now have a new respect for elk and moose antlers. Conversation after conversation, I learned new things about people from all over the world.

We had our last dinner on the cruise with a couple, and the conversations started like many others during the cruise. But I quickly realized they only communicated with my wife, not me. When I would say something, they did not turn to face me and didn't even look like they heard me!

I tried talking louder, but still, they did not seem to know I was there. I tried participating a few more times in the conversation, yet the woman sitting opposite me and the man sitting to my right continued just to engage with my wife.

Frustration quickly got replaced with wonder. What adventures can I have with the power of invisibility?

I disengaged from the dinner conversation and focused on the bread and butter in the middle of our table. Can I touch all the bread pieces in the bread bowl before making my selection? Can I take all of the ornately carved butter pieces in the dish and roll them into a large butterball? Other equally evil dinner experiments, some involving inappropriate sounds, popped into my head throughout the rest of dinner and way into dessert.

While considering deflating the woman's lemon souffle with my pinky, I realized no one was talking. My wife repeated the question the woman asked me. "Steve, what do you do for work?"

I was so shocked that my invisibility superpower had faded that I stumbled out, "Oh, I work with data. Always have." And that was it. I had lost the opportunity to educate this couple on the benefits of data modeling.

After dinner, my wife and I walked on the deck. "You were quiet tonight," she said.

I whispered back, "I was invisible."

November

I love Halloween. Although I miss the crisp New Jersey air with crunching leaves and trick-or-treating excitement, the high desert of Arizona has its own Halloween magic. Last week, a group of us in Sedona hiked over five miles by the light of the full moon–and in costumes! We didn't see anyone else the entire hike, but if we did, they would run the other way when they saw several skeletons, a donkey, and a hot air balloon approaching. (I was the hot air balloon.)

For the Day of the Dead, we joined a group sitting around a bonfire in the courtyard of our library and shared stories about departed family members and friends.

The evening mystique of the fire and candle-lit lanterns, combined with the librarian's Irish accent and Celtic garb, transported me back over a thousand years to an open farm pasture in Ireland.

The librarian shared stories of a close friend and then told Celtic myths about life and death. I jumped in with a couple of stories about my dad. The woman sitting with a dog on her lap on the other side of the bonfire shared a story about her brother.

The woman next to her told a story of a friend, and then, as we started roasting marshmallows, she added that she is becoming quite skilled at talking to animals, and started a conversation with the dog on the woman's lap beside her. As she revealed to us there is a cat in the neighborhood that the dog befriended, I realized I was no longer in ancient Ireland but back in present-day weird Sedona.

Time to go home and eat some Halloween candy!

December

It was a warm summer beach day, and my older sister and I ran back to my mom to show her our completed art projects. Even though I was barely six, I clearly remember the soup bowl-sized circles we colored in with magic markers, bordered by rolled-up blue, red, and yellow crepe paper. My mom was talking to a teacher friend when we arrived half out of breath. My mom commented on how colorful they were. Her teacher friend added, "This is beautiful," she said, looking at my sister's work. She then looked at mine and quietly added, "It's amazing how different both of these are."

I never had the patience for art. Throughout middle school, I had the same art teacher as my sister. My art teacher beamed when he first met me in seventh grade, commenting on my sister's skills and looking forward to seeing my creations. After our first assignment, I think we both realized I should have taken gym instead of art.

However, my solution to not being artistic was to focus on quantity. If he gave a class assignment to paint a picture of a skyscraper, I painted the entire New York City skyline (poorly, though). For our Halloween assignment, I turned in not one drawing but five. If we had to create abstract art with a handful of cotton balls, I used an entire bag of cotton balls.

My quantity-over-quality approach to art surprisingly worked. At my middle school graduation, out of hundreds of better-qualified candidates, I received the sole Art Award. My friends were shocked…and so was I, as I walked up on stage to receive my certificate.

Our library had a painting session last week. My wife convinced me to go, and we painted with watercolor on small canvas pallets at a large round table with some locals.

It was no surprise that I finished before everyone else at our large table. The man painting beside me admired my wife's partially completed artwork and commented on how it truly captured the Arizona winter landscape. Then he glanced at mine. "That's interesting," he said.

I did mention to him and everyone else at the table that I won the art award in middle school. People nodded and went back to their projects. I paused for a moment, then got up and went to the front of the room to grab a handful of empty canvases.

"Quantity over quality," I told myself as I squeezed out some more paint on my paper plate pallet.

2024

January

We recently vacationed in the "Land of the Long White Cloud." Mother Nature was definitely having a good day when she created New Zealand. The mountains, waterfalls, lakes, birds, flowers—so beautiful!

While off-roading through hairpin turns and up and down terrain that made my teeth chatter, a large spider landed on our younger daughter. "Almost completely harmless," our guide said of this Herdsmen spider. He then added that no animals can kill you in New Zealand.

In the absence of dangerous animals, there are dangerous activities.

We took a boat ride in the Doubtful Sound, and our captain steered his boat within inches of sheer rock cliffs so we could look directly up at a waterfall. We did a jet boat ride where we exceeded 50 miles per hour in ankle-deep water. They locked us in a freezing room at the Antarctic Museum that simulated an Antarctic wind storm (I now no longer need to travel to Antarctica—cross that off my list!).

These are just some of the crazy activities that made me realize that in addition to having no dangerous animals in this country, New Zealand also has no personal injury attorneys! So much adventure!

Our last adventure was white water rafting. After rafting at Pennsylvania's Delaware Water Gap, I assumed rafting involved some floating but mostly a can of beer in one hand and dragging the raft over rocks with the other hand—slow going and relaxing. I expected the same lazy river-type experience here. Instead, it was Class 5 rapids right from the beginning. There were at least ten large drops, including the largest commercial rafting drop in the world - over 21 feet!

After surviving each drop, our guide would say enthusiastically, "Happy Days!" I am not sure what this phrase means after facing the full wrath of the river again and again. Our older daughter was chosen to sit on the edge of the front of the boat, barely hanging on for a ten-foot drop over the falls. After we fished her out of the water, our guide said again, "Happy Days!" Scary adventures!

My last activity of the trip, however, was the scariest. I decided not to work hard and take it easy during this vacation. I usually work at least four hours a day while on holiday, but on this vacation, I worked just enough to keep up with emails. This last activity was writing my "to do" list. Five pages full of tasks for the upcoming week!

Now that's scary!

February

I decided to surprise my wife for her birthday a few weeks back. I got up before her and drove to the nearest supermarket to get her a bouquet of flowers. Being out of practice buying flowers (I think I used to buy her flowers regularly - what happened?), made me feel overwhelmed as I stared at bins and bins of flowers.

"Bing." The text, from my wife, contained no words, just a picture of a bouquet of flowers on sale at the Whole Foods down the road. I returned to my car, realizing the flowers would no longer be a surprise. I really wanted to surprise her!

Whole Foods had very few flowers left, and they appeared to be sold out of the flowers on sale. I found a similar-looking bouquet, but it rang up at full price at the register.

After talking to three employees, I learned that no more bouquets were on sale. I picked up a large bouquet with a glass vase and asked if they could price match this, as these flowers "look half dead anyway."

This was probably not a nice comment to make about their flowers, but all of their flowers looked like someone had forgotten to water them…for a month. After a few minutes of negotiating with the flower man at Whole Foods, I could see he was getting flustered. He finally said, "Why don't you just take one of these bouquets for free," and handed me a large bouquet of similar-looking half-dead flowers.

I wanted to thank him for the free shriveled flowers, but when I looked up, he was gone.

I then used the money I saved on flowers to buy a brownie mix for a birthday cake and also some organic strawberries.

As I was driving home, I took a deep breath and smiled, inhaling the faint smell of strawberries and decaying flowers, and realized that my wife receiving a bouquet of wilted flowers would surprise her after all!

March

I sometimes wonder what mom and dad birds feel when their last fledging leaves the nest. Are they happy and can't wait to finally migrate to Hawaii? Or are they at loose ends, wishing for frequent visits from their chicks?

Last semester, our youngest left for college. Since her college is only an hour away, she came home almost every weekend.

We went for hikes, garage sales, and out for dinners. This semester, however, she finally found "her people" and plans fun activities almost every night. She has been home for a handful of weekends this semester, but she is always excited to return to school.

"I need to be back early Sunday to watch a lacrosse game," she said last weekend when she visited.

I am happy that both of our kids are mostly independent. But I am also happy when they come back home to the "nest" to see us old birds.

Or, on second thought, maybe migrating to Hawaii is not such a bad idea…

April

Two weeks ago, I took our younger daughter to get her wisdom teeth extracted. (The word 'extracted' always makes me shiver.) The protocol when we arrived was similar to any dentist visit until the nurse asked us to watch a movie. She hit a few buttons on the keyboard and left the room as a movie started playing on the monitor. I love movies!

Over the next five minutes, the movie explained in way too much detail all the things that could go wrong during wisdom teeth surgery. This was not an entertaining flick—it was a horror film! I tried to block out most of it, but phrases like "hole into nasal cavity," "cracked jaw," and "fatal" were hard to ignore.

After the short film, the nurse returned to our room smiling and escorted me half-dazed from the movie into the waiting room. Luckily, I brought some data modeling work with me but couldn't concentrate because they played that movie's soundtrack the entire time I was in the waiting room—over and over!

Then, a few days later, I went for an eye exam. Every eye test I took was like a video game. The first game was clicking a button whenever a flicker appeared on the screen. After blasting at least 20 squiggly lines, I looked up from the screen and noticed a frown on the assistant's face. "You missed quite a few."

"Can I take it again?" I said, trying to hide the worry in my voice. I played the game two more times and bombed each time.

When I met with the eye doctor, he saw my scores and recommended I play an additional "game" after lunch. This machine occupied its own room and looked scary, but I told myself it is just another video game. Since the little dot was very faint and appeared and disappeared rapidly, I just kept clicking the button. This strategy worked for me in Galaga—as long as I have unlimited fire power, it should work here too. (I must have clicked that button a thousand times over the 24-minute test.) I didn't want to lose this game, thinking a low score would surely lead to me having some serious eye issues.

I have learned from these two experiences to never trust a movie or game in any doctor's office!

May

I opened the envelope postmarked from England where my friend was spending a college semester abroad. The trip agenda inside detailed where we would stay and how we would travel during our one-week, six-country, budget-friendly whirlwind tour of Europe. Our spring breaks aligned, so in just a few short weeks, I would fly to England

and together we would see as much as we could with our unlimited teenage energy.

I recall my favorite parts of this trip were the "in betweens." For example, I'm glad I saw the Eiffel Tower in Paris and the Grossmünster Church in Zurich, but it was so much fun taking the overnight train ride from Paris to Zurich. This train ride was the "in between"—connecting the dots between trip highlights.

Time flew: undergraduate degree, graduate degree, job 1, job 2, marriage, job 3, dog 1, child 1, child 2, more jobs, dog 2; Reagon, Bush, Clinton, George W., Obama, Trump, Biden; WTO, Y2K, 9/11, SARS, FOMC, H1N1, COVID-19; Indiana, Aladdin, Neo, Potter, Aragorn, Sparrow, Anakin, Gru, Katniss, Wade…and, phew, after 36 years, my friend and I returned to Europe.

Two weeks ago, the four of us (our wives and us) went to Portugal. It was different, though.

Instead of the adrenalin rush to see as much as possible, we opted for three-hour dinners, long walks, and scenic drives off the motorways. We traded the overnight train ride and hostels for comfy inns and even one night in a castle. Forget that used travel book covering all of Europe! We chose private guided walking tours.

However, just like that first trip to Europe, the "in betweens" were the most fun. Exploring the ruins of a castle late at night in a "stop-over" town between two major cities, getting lost while trekking through vineyards to fill an early afternoon while waiting for a tour to start, and scouring supermarket shelves for vegan lunch snacks to sneak into a museum.

I am already looking forward to the next European trip with the four of us in 2060!

June

I love going to garage sales. I completely forget about the entire world and all senses focus on the glitter and garbage surrounding me. We spend the summers in New Jersey, and once a year, our small town has a townwide garage sale. It was this Saturday, and I biked to over 50 garage sales—three hours of pure fun.

After morning pleasantries, I always ask the same question to the garage sale host: "Do you have any old cards for sale?"

I collect old baseball and other kinds of cards—"old" means older than me. I've always started off with this question at sales, even as a kid going to garage sales with my family.

If I were to group all the answers I have received over the last fifty years to this question, 99.9% of the answers would start with "No," or "Sorry," followed by "My parents threw them away," "Never got into collecting stuff," or "I'm saving them for my kids (or grandkids)."

Roughly one out of a thousand garage sales though, the answer is "Yes," or "I think so, let me check." Once, after asking this question when I was about 12 years old, I was rewarded with a shoebox of baseball cards from the 1960s (including several Mickey Mantles)—all for $5!

Sometimes, though, as I amass more and more cards in drawers and filing cabinets, a scary one-word question pops into my head: "Why?"

My kids (and most younger people) have no interest in collecting old stuff, and sometimes I am reminded, even by well-meaning garage sale hosts, "You can't take it with you."

But it's not in the owning but in the finding, isn't it? In a previous life, I imagine I could have been a gold prospector, rare orchid hunter, or pearl diver. In fact, I'm already planning the garage sales to visit this Saturday!

July

I recently bought two Roomba vacuum cleaners at a garage sale. These round and sleek robot vacuums were still in their original boxes, and the seller told me they both worked. After giving each a name, I charged Ernie and Bert overnight in their docking stations. The next day, I pressed the Clean button on Ernie, and he cautiously moved forward a few inches and then slowly moved to the right and then the right again, creating almost a perfect circle. He proceeded to travel in that same very small circle…around again and again. Several minutes passed before Ernie froze and, after a moment of silence, played Taps from its speakers.

Before troubleshooting Ernie, I pressed Clean on Bert. Bert went fairly fast in a straight line for several feet before pausing and then playing that same sad song.

I watched a few YouTube videos and spent over an hour troubleshooting the units, including cleaning all of the sensors, filing the corroded battery connections, and taking apart and reconnecting the brushes.

After another evening of charging, I set both off to clean our floor.

Just like the day before, Bert took off and proceeded to go in a circle, but this time, even faster than before. After a few minutes of cleaning and recleaning the same circle, Bert fired off Taps and expired.

Ernie, perhaps sensing that it might be the last time to prove himself, took off with gusto and zoomed down the hallway.

I have never seen a robot vacuum move so fast!

It then turned around and rushed back, stopping a few feet in front of me, was quiet for a moment (catching its breath?), and played its last rendition of taps.

You can imagine what happened next. I'll give you a hint, garbage pickup was the next day. Both Ernie and Bert joined the giant vacuum heaven in the sky.

I feel though that Ernie and Bert were trying to impart upon me some valuable lessons. Maybe they were trying to make the point that when the seller said they both "work," I should have clarified what "work" actually meant. Going in a circle or straight line for several minutes can pass for "work." Maybe Ernie was showing the value of doing a very small task extremely well (that tiny circle was clean after all!).

But I know in my heart the best lesson they both taught me: never buy a used vacuum cleaner!

August

Dig deeper! More sand at the castle base! A big wave is coming! My brother and I continue to shout commands as we reinforce our sand castle while waves fill the moats and batter the castle's walls.

Waves keep coming, sandcastles erect and dissolve, and days, months, years, and decades pass like sand through our fingers. Roughly five decades later, during this past weekend, we returned to building sandcastles at the beach. My brother and I, along with two of his kids, yelled to each other over the sounds of the waves what to do, while piling sand and digging trenches.

Sandcastle building is about as Zen as you can get! The simple goal of keeping the castle in tact is a complete sensory experience—the smell of cool ocean air, the sound of crashing and sizzling waves, the feel of wet handfuls of sand and cold ocean water rushing over ankles, the taste of salt, the sight of the current wave stretching for the castle walls and giving up while the next wave roars and charges towards us.

Sandcastle building keeps you in the moment—no room for worry or stress. Politics, climate change, health, work, social media, AI, investments, traffic…all fight for mental attention but lose when we're in the moment.

After lunch, I walked back to the ocean and noticed little sand bumps where our proud castle stood. I would like to say that profound thoughts popped into my head: Are the means more important than the ends? Is the process what matters? Nothing is permanent, it's the moments that count. Instead, I wondered how Nvidia will do this upcoming week and about the beach traffic waiting for us on the Long Island Expressway for the ride home.

Where's the beach shovel when you need it?

September

When you picture the Jersey Shore, picture our neighbor. He is loud with every other sentence containing at least one word of profanity, quick with dirty jokes, and I have seen him in a shirt only twice in the last 15 summers. He makes the best pizza (with homemade Italian sauce) and the most delicious Zeppole (donut-like balls drowned in powdered sugar). If you ever eat more than three of his Zeppole in one sitting, you won't be hungry for the rest of the summer (I had seven Zeppole during our last visit). His house is always full of neighbors, kids, grandkids, and friends.

He had a massive party one Saturday during our first summer at the shore. There must have been over 50 people, almost all men around his age. People started arriving in the early afternoon, and the party continued until way after midnight. At one point, the raucous quieted, and I looked out my bedroom window and saw the group take a picture behind a large school sign.

The next day, our neighbor told us that he went to an all-male high school in Bayonne, and every year, he invites his entire class to his house for a party. His friends travel from as far away as Florida to attend. It was his 52nd high school reunion.

The following year, it was almost equally loud. Again, the classmates took a picture behind that sign.

Over the years, it has become quieter and quieter.

This summer, I watched again as the group, now less than 20, smiled and held up the sign. I was outside watching the photo shoot when my neighbor saw me and shouted, "Want a f**ken beer?" (Replace these asterisks to spell an expletive.)

I nodded and he walked over with two ice-cold beers (one for me and one for my wife).

Sometimes, I'll try to picture my neighbor as the CFO of one of the largest financial companies in the world. I would like to ask him what made him not go to work in his lavish office on one of the higher floors of the Twin Towers on 9/11 (when almost his whole department did go into work that day), but that would be a serious conversation, and I don't think I've ever had a conversation with my neighbor that didn't end with me laughing.

If life is like one of those cheesy carnival games on the Jersey Shore boardwalk, how would you win that grand prize? You know, that huge stuffed alien that you don't have a place for anyway. Is it based on how many quarters you have, or on how many times you make people laugh, the number of parties you host, or the quantity of Zeppole you make for others?

I think my neighbor would win the f**ken prize.

October

We just got back from an Alaskan cruise and had dinner almost every night with different people. I look for inspiration during these conversations. For example, take Pat, a retired farmer from Spokane, who said after we learned that he and his wife were staying in the largest suite on the ship: "We're going to keep going until we go broke or get broken!" Andrew is slowly losing his eyesight, and he and his wife are doing as many cruises as possible before he loses his vision completely (six more cruises booked before the end of this year!). Keri and her husband had been looking forward to this cruise for a while. Her husband died a few months before the cruise, so she decided to go solo, the first time traveling alone after 45 years of marriage.

A common theme? Carpe diem!

We actually "seized the day" during the cruise. One partly cloudy night (the only night it didn't rain—so much rain in Alaska!), the ship's cruise director announced that there was a very small chance to see the Northern Lights. In the spirit of seizing the day, we got up at 1 am, put on warm clothes, and pushed the deck door open against the heavy wind into the icy Alaskan air. I knew we were in for a treat when those already on the deck had their iPhones pointed to the night sky. Lots of green spirals of color in the sky—amazing!

Carpe diem!

November

Have you ever played pickleball? If you have, you know that pickleball is the best sport ever invented. Like most sports, it is great exercise and good for the mind. However, pickleball has several advantages over other sports. There is a short learning curve to become proficient (just hit the ball over the net!), yet you can continually get better and better. It does not take up much space to play (you are playing on a space half the size of a tennis court or three times the size of a ping pong table). Nothing beats the sound of the paddle making contact with the pickleball. And what a language—dink, pickled, poach, banger, and more!

My wife and I started playing during Covid. We needed an outdoor activity that was also social. Early on, there were maybe 20 people who would show up at the local tennis court, and we would set up our own nets and play over cracked asphalt. But the sport keeps growing, even in our small town. Last year, our town built 12 new pickleball courts, which are always full, and sometimes, over 50 people are waiting to play on weekends!

Although pickleball is amazing, here's what baffles me about the sport. I can trail run eight miles and not be sore the next day, but if I play even an hour of pickleball, I will be sore for a week! And it's just hitting a small plastic ball back and forth on a tiny court!

Also, I wish pickleball had a tougher-sounding name. When people see me limping and I tell them it is because of pickleball, it just doesn't sound so good. We need a more punishing-sounding name for the sport—maybe a name that contains terms like "iron," "crush," or "mixed martial arts"?

Or maybe I just stick to trail running…

December

When I was little, I loved going to baseball card shows. My dad would take me to a few every year, including once to a large one in Manhattan. If you've never been to a baseball card show, imagine a dated hotel meeting space filled with the hum of mostly middle-aged men chatting around tables about selling, buying, and trading cards. If you took a deep breath (and I don't recommend taking too many of these within the show), you would smell a combination of musty cardboard, hotdogs, and high school gym locker room.

There's also always electricity in the air with the excitement of getting a great deal.

Missing these smells and excitement, I decided to take a table and become a vendor at a small show in Phoenix. The timing seemed right, as I could get rid of some of my cards, and I also now fit in that middle-aged demographic. I asked my friend (who also fits the demographic) to join me. With his crazy schedule of running a healthcare facility, I was surprised when he texted back right away with, "That would be super fun!"

I picked him up early this past Saturday, and we drove to Phoenix with a car full of cards and other memorabilia.

For the whole drive, we talked about cards and how we would arrange our six-foot table to maximize displaying everything. I don't remember the last time I talked about something so trivial for so long, but it felt great!

The show was mostly outside (great time of year to be in Phoenix), and after we set up our table, I looked around and realized that my friend and I were probably the oldest vendors. Most were young people selling cards I knew little about, like Pokémon and Magic.

My friend brought merchandise that was perfect for the audience, and within two hours, he made many sales, and his side of our table was getting emptier and emptier.

On the other hand, my side was just like it was when I set up. I brought cards I like to collect but quickly found out nobody there even knew about these cards. "What are these?" more than one passerby asked. Some stopped to browse.

A girl in her twenties went through a stack of animal cards and found one she loved. "I have a thing for lemurs," she said, beaming, holding up one of the cards containing a strange-looking furry animal that I guessed was a lemur. I was about to explain the history of the series containing that card, that this series was from 1909 and the printing used back then was state-of-the-art and still surpasses printing today in some ways. Instead, I said, hoping she would quickly move on to the next table, "Take that card as a gift."

Several other bizarre collecting habits throughout the day led to me giving away even more cards. One person, with the striking appearance of a motorcycle gang leader, even forced me to take a dollar for a hummingbird card that I wanted to give him for free. He spent almost an hour going through all of my cards, looking for one that contained a hummingbird. Nobody else came by my table during this time (maybe they were afraid of him). He said he wanted a hummingbird card for his mother, who is so gentle that when she goes outside, hummingbirds flock to her. I tried hard to picture a flock of hummingbirds.

After several other conversations completely outside my comfort zone, I realized this might be my last card show, at least for a while. My friend sold over $1,000 in cards. I made $30 but gave over $50 in cards for free. Although I am not a math expert, I think my time is better spent just buying cards instead of selling them.

Or maybe just selling lemur and hummingbird cards…

Life Tactics

What works

When we first took our older daughter to the beach, we plopped her down in her diaper on the wet sand near the waves. We surrounded her with plastic beach toys, including a shovel, pail, and rake. Before picking up the shovel, she pushed her hand down into the wet sand and, not knowing what it was, put her hand in her mouth. She made a face I think I captured in a video somewhere, and she never ate sand again.

A few summers later, we took our daughters out for ice cream. Our younger daughter fussed in her stroller while our toddler took a spoonful of chocolate ice cream and offered it to her younger sister. This was the first time our younger daughter tasted ice cream. Her eyes widened and she opened her mouth again, wanting another spoonful of that cold sweet treat.

Life is trial and error. If something doesn't work, we try not to do it again. No more eating sand. If something works well, we try to repeat it. More chocolate ice cream, please!

Over the last five-plus decades, I have tried approaches and techniques that sometimes are gritty like sand and sometimes taste like chocolate ice cream. This chapter summarizes ten tactics that taste like chocolate ice cream—they work for me.

I hope you find at least one approach or technique that works for you and can make today better (more productive, more meaningful, and more laughs).

Do "to do"

1	Finish writing the introduction to my book.
2	Edit Chapter 4 of Doug's book.
3	Schedule next trip to NY to see mom.

Stop reading for a moment and think of everything you need to do before the end of the day. Phew!

When we think about all of the activities we need to complete, our present task (whether work-related or fun) suffers as we are no longer in the present. Also, it is stressful thinking about the future, even if it is just a few minutes ahead of the present—so much to do!

Write down all of the activities you need to complete. It could be for work or fun; it could be a high-level goal or a detailed task; it could require completing today or by next Friday; it could require five minutes to perform or 15 hours.

Use pencils and paper, Microsoft Word, Google Docs, or a phone app.

In addition to helping you focus on the current activity, a "to do" list feels great when you remove a completed task.

Here is my list for today (I'll limit it to ten to save space):

1. Finish writing this book.

2. Edit Doug's book. [We publish books on data, and I edit most of them myself.]

3. Research how to get rid of cliff chipmunks without hurting them. [They are cute but destructive.]

4. Buy Nvidia stock?

5. Call the Bright Angel Lodge to see if there's a cancellation. [This places books over a year in advance but sometimes has a last-minute cancellation.]

6. Schedule next trip to NY to see family.

7. Book hotel for robotics conference. [I love robots.]

8. Did we receive a refund from booking.com from canceling hotel?

9. Backup website.

10. Get oil change.

What are the "Top Three" highest priority items on your list? The high-priority items are those that you need to work on today. Only pick three. This forces you to not waste time doing silly activities. It also makes you aware that your time is so important.

Here are my "Top 3" in terms of priority:

1. Finish writing this book.

2. Edit Doug's book.

3. Schedule next trip to NY to see mom.

The other items don't disappear, though. To use a baseball analogy, they are in the bullpen waiting to go on deck. You can list them as a bullet list below the "Top Three" if they also have to get done today. If you use a Calendar application, you can move those items that don't have to get done today to tomorrow or the next day. For example, I can get the oil change tomorrow, so I move that task a day out on my calendar. The other items I will list below in the same document:

1	Finish writing this book.
2	Edit Doug's book.
3	Schedule next trip to NY to see mom.

- Research how to get rid of cliff chipmunks without hurting them.
- Buy Nvidia stock?
- Call the Bright Angel Lodge to see if there's a cancellation.
- Book hotel for robotics conference.
- Did we receive refund from booking.com from canceling hotel?
- Backup website.

I like a bullet list instead of a numbered list for these lower-priority items because the numbered list implies a priority, and I don't know yet which items to work on next.

I love this tiny three-row spreadsheet! I have used this spreadsheet since 1990 to manage over 12,000 of my days and easily over 250,000 tasks!

Now, start completing the items on your list. Once you complete an item, remove it from the list and move the others up. So, for example, once I finished writing this book, this would now be my spreadsheet:

1	Edit Doug's book.
2	Schedule next trip to NY to see mom.
3	

I would then take the next most important item on my list and put it in for #3:

1	Edit Doug's book.
2	Schedule next trip to NY to see mom.
3	Backup website.

So we have these rolling three sets of tasks. Once one completes, move the other two up and add a third. That's it!

Recall our original list:

1	Finish writing this book.
2	Edit Doug's book.
3	Schedule next trip to NY to see mom.

Often, we add big items such as #1. There is no way I can finish writing this book before editing Doug's book. Not only would Doug get upset and never write another book for us again, but I would miss the opportunity to see my mom in New York.

So, how do you eat an elephant? One bite at a time. (I'm not too crazy about this quote because I like elephants and I'm a vegan, but you get the idea.) Break huge projects down into smaller ones.

We need to make sure our activities are doable within a short amount of time. If it takes too long to complete, we either skip it or keep working away to the detriment of the other tasks. Although sometimes we need to keep working on a task until it is done (even if it takes all day or longer), we can usually break it down into small pieces. For example:

1	Finish writing the introduction to my book.
2	Edit Chapter 4 of Doug's book.
3	Schedule next trip to NY to see mom.

The first two activities are now smaller and more doable. Although there are always exceptions, I try to list items that take less than a few hours to complete. After completing one item, I might add the next-most-important item to complete from the bullet list below this spreadsheet, add another chapter of Doug's book to edit, or add another section of my book to work on.

In addition, sometimes I might be working on one activity when an email or phone call reprioritizes that work, or I might complete the third activity before the first due to a quick conversation with a colleague.

My "to do" list allows me to plan well and be incredibly productive each day. It also takes a lot of stress out of the day. In fact, it makes my days more like a game, seeing how much I can actually complete and remove in a given day.

I started my first "to do" list over 35 years ago in Microsoft Word for Windows 1.1, and today it runs on Office 365 and Windows 11, but the basic structure is the same. Use it too!

Use the "to do" list and you will be amazed at how much you can accomplish!

Play the crane game

Did you ever play the crane game? Put money in the machine and maneuver a crane with a joystick above potential prizes to win. Once you align the crane directly above your desired prize, push the button, and the crane slowly goes down and attempts to scoop it up and deposit it in a chute for your retrieval.

Our daughters enjoyed playing this game at the Seaside boardwalk on the Jersey Shore. Although luck plays a factor in winning, there is also some skill. You have to position the crane over the desired prize and not be distracted by the many other prizes nearby that are also vying for your attention.

The crane game requires mental focus and concentration.

When our younger daughter was in middle school, she would share some of her school worries with us, usually before going to bed.

I needed to find a way to explain to her that we can't control the stream of thoughts that pop in and out of our heads—that's just how our brains work. As the meditation books say, we can't control our stream of thoughts any more than controlling and calming the ocean waves.

However, we can control which thoughts to pick up, think more about, and let the other thoughts be. Let those thoughts we don't care for come and go, pop in and out, enter and leave, and eventually disappear for good.

Just like the crane game! We can't control what prizes (thoughts) lie below our crane, all vying for our attention, but we can control which thoughts we want to "pick up."

This analogy with the crane game seemed to help our younger daughter a lot. You don't have control over which prizes are available, just like you don't have control over the stream of thoughts that pop in and out of our heads. However, just like you can maneuver that crane over the prize of your choice, you can also decide which thoughts to pick up and which to ignore.

Have your crane pick up the prizes that keep you in the present, make you happy, and get the most out of your days.

Identify your gifts

> *The meaning of life is to find your gift. The purpose of life is to give it away.*
>
> Shakespeare

If Shakespeare is right about life, what is your gift (or gifts)?

For example, one of my gifts is endurance.

In elementary school, I collected baseball cards like many of my friends. My favorite part of owning the cards was organizing them. I would sort each card until over 500 were stacked sequentially. Today, I still collect cards and have sorted thousands of them, one at a time.

I can take a small task and do it again and again, for close to forever.

I can take one step and then another and eventually run for hours. I can drive a mile and then another and eventually drive across the country.

I can write a single word and then another and eventually complete a 50,000-word book on data modeling. When someone reads my book, they can improve their skills.

I can create a single PowerPoint slide of a technique I want to teach and then another slide. Today, I teach a 20-hour data modeling class with over 600 PowerPoint slides. Attendees of my class can better their careers.

When I write books and teach my classes, I am sharing my gift with others ("giving it away").

What is your gift (or gifts) and how can it help others?

Stretch

Did you ever ride one of those nineteenth-century carousels? The hand-painted horses and lions revolve around a large organ booming carnival tunes.

Nunley's Amusement Park on Long Island had one of these 1880s carousels. Near the carousel was a long red chute filled with metal rings. As the carousel went around, you could stretch all the way out and try to grab a ring from the chute.

If your arms were long enough and you were fast enough, you could actually grab multiple rings in one pass.

All of the rings were silver except for one that was gold. It was probably made of brass or copper, but as a kid, I thought it was solid gold. If you were lucky enough to grab the gold ring, you would get a free ride on the carousel.

Being little, I could barely reach the rings, and if I did ever get one, it was always silver. I always remember stretching for those rings. I never gave up trying to get the gold ring. We need to always stretch for things that are difficult to obtain or outside our comfort zone.

For example, as kids, our family used to go to a swimming pool with a very high diving board. I remember grabbing the cold and wet stainless steel poles, one in each hand, and climbing up over 30 steps. I was scared to be so high above the water. But I walked to the end of the narrow and bouncy diving board…and jumped. This was a stretch.

About 15 years after my last jump off that board, I was sitting in a large meeting room as about a hundred of us data professionals waited to hear a presentation from a well-known speaker in my field. As the minutes ticked away, the person who organized this meeting, who was a friend of mine, whispered to me that the speaker called and said he could not make the meeting. "What do we do?" she asked, close to a state of panic.

"I can speak," I said, not sure whose voice just said this. She was surprised I volunteered, but within a few minutes, I was introduced, and there I was, standing in front of a room of data people, where I was definitely the youngest. I pictured walking to the end of that diving board and jumping, just as I opened my mouth to speak in front of that room.

I started talking about a challenge I was facing at work related to data and asked attendees about their experiences. I facilitated a 90-minute discussion on this topic, sharing my thoughts, listening to those of the attendees, and summarizing the key takeaways. I heard feedback later that the talk was one of their best. This is another example of stretching.

One of my favorite stories that reminds me of stretching is from Danaan Parry's, "Warriors of the Heart - A Handbook for Conflict Resolution":

> *Sometimes, I feel my life is a series of trapeze swings. I'm either hanging on to a trapeze bar swinging along or, for a few moments, I'm hurtling across space between the trapeze bars.*

Mostly, I spend my time hanging on for dear life, to the trapeze bar of the moment. It carries me along a certain steady rate of swing and I have the feeling that I am in control. I know most of the right questions, and even some of the right answers. But once in a while, as I'm merrily, or not so merrily, swinging along, I look ahead of me into the distance, and what do I see?

I see another trapeze bar looking at me. It's empty; and I know that this new bar has my name on it. It is my next step, my growth, my aliveness coming to get me. In my heart-of-hearts I know that for me to grow, I must release my grip on the present well-known bar, to move to the new one.

Each time it happens, I hope—no, I pray—that I won't have to grab the new one. But deep down I know that I must totally release my grasp on my old bar, and for some moments in time I must hurtle across space before I can grab the new bar. Each time I am filled with terror. It doesn't even matter that in all my previous hurtles I've always made it.

Each time, I am afraid I will miss, that I will be crushed on unseen rocks in the bottomless basin between the bars. But I do it anyway. I must.

We need to always challenge ourselves and reach for that gold ring or grab for that next trapeze.

Stretch!

Learn then leverage

I am not a good sailor, but I know the basic rules around wind. After flipping five times on my little Sunfish last summer in the Barnegat Bay, I know one rule is that I should probably not sail.

Our older daughter is a great sailor. She is president of her sailing team at Arizona State, practices several days a week, and participates in many regattas throughout the school year. I have watched a few of the regattas, and am always so impressed that these college kids can sail in any direction they need to with respect to the wind, even backward sometimes to "park" their boats. They definitely know how to use the wind to their advantage.

It takes more than just knowing the rules of the wind to win a regatta, though. The eventual winner may need to be resourceful sometimes, cutting in front of other sailboats or "stealing the wind" from those boats nearby.

So, learning the basic rules of sailing can make you a good sailor, and leveraging this information and your experiences (and others' experiences) can make you a great sailor.

Sailing is a system. A system is a container (a subset of life) that uses rules to function in a certain way. Learn the system and do well. Leverage or bend the system and do even better. Think of those sailors who can leverage the wind, and sometimes, it requires being opportune to finish first.

Learning how a system works can help you survive and maybe succeed. Leveraging a system can make you excel (and help others too!).

We get exposed to systems at an early age. A classroom is a system, for example. Arrive on time and pay attention during class and do well. Study extra for exams or know who to study with (or who to sit next to) and do very well.

Realize systems are all around us. For example, next time you travel, think about the system in place at hotels to check guests in. Once you learn the system, you can get your room key and get settled in your room. Leverage the system, and you can get a free room upgrade or complimentary access to the hotel's lounge.

Systems contain systems, each with its own rules and opportunities for gain.

The hotel is a system within a city. The city is a system within a country. The city contains a system of roads, and we adapt to the roads by following traffic rules, such as stopping at red traffic lights, driving the proper way down one-way streets, and sticking close to speed limits. Each city and country contains thousands of systems.

There are lots of systems we are part of every day. Society is probably the broadest. We act as citizens within the boundaries of society. We need to act and perform a certain way to make society work. We cannot, for example, keep driving the wrong way down a one-way street and not expect some consequences. We cannot wait on the "ten or less" item at the supermarket with a shopping cart filled to the brim and not expect some consequences. We cannot talk at full volume in a library and not expect some consequences. And so on.

So be aware that systems are all around us, and the most successful know how to leverage them!

Ask

Author Nora Roberts once said, "If you don't ask, the answer is no."

My mom always reminds us of this quote. We all have things we want or need, and it is ok to ask for them. If someone says "no," we are no worse off than not asking in the first place.

If you want a free upgrade, ask.

If you want to ask him out, ask.

If you want the corner office, ask.

Sometimes, society labels asking as aggressive or selfish. And sometimes, people can ask in ways where these labels are justified.

For example, "Would it be possible to request a complimentary upgrade?" is a much more pleasant question than the more aggressive and demanding, "Give me an upgrade!"

So, ask for what you want. If the answer is "no," you are no worse off. And if "yes," all the better!

Go veg

Don't you hate when people tell you what to eat?

Ok then, let's keep this one short.

Eat plants. A plant-based diet (vegan) means you can eat anything except for food containing animals, dairy, or eggs. What's left? Many amazing foods, and more, it seems every day, as food companies produce healthier foods that are kinder to animals and the environment.

It's challenging to make a change and what makes going vegan even harder is that our culture and government continue to promote the unhealthy diet of consuming dead animals and cow's milk. Even with our friends and family, you might receive questions like, "How can you just eat plants? Where do you get your iron, amino acids, protein, omegas, and B12?"

Plants can give you more of what you need and more. I am just sharing my thoughts and full disclaimer, I am not a health professional. I read some great books, though, like *The China Study* by Thomas M. Campbell II and T. Colin Campbell, and *Eat and Run* by Scott Jurek. Also, there are some compelling movies and YouTube videos to watch. A plant-based diet might give you these benefits (it did for me):

- More energy
- Fewer colds and other illnesses
- Sharper mind
- Cleaner conscious
- Better digestion
- Sounder sleep

Try a vegan diet (or even a vegetarian diet) for one day a week, a week, a month, or longer, and see how you feel!

Travel

Think of at least five happy memories, and I bet at least two happened while on vacation.

I love traveling. I enjoy seeing things from a different perspective, experiencing each day at a refreshing pace that differs from the usual routine, and talking with the locals.

I no longer crave snapping pictures of the "must-see" attractions like the Eiffel Tower in Paris or the largest ball of yarn in Kansas. Instead, I seek the salty smell of an ocean, the yelling and crowds of an outdoor market, and the views along a "locals-only" hiking trail.

It doesn't have to be far. It can even be in the next town.

So plan your next trip and make some happy memories!

Act like the expert

My first business trip! I've only been out of graduate school for a few months, but my manager asked me to deliver a data modeling presentation at Southwestern Bell in St. Louis.

There were over 50 IT professionals, and I knew these attendees' average years of experience with data management and telecommunications was greater than my age. In other words, I was the least experienced person in the room by decades.

My graduate school program was intense—14 months of advanced electrical engineering and computer science classes at Carnegie Mellon University. I took an acting class to reduce the stress from this program and also to have some fun. Carnegie Mellon has one of the best acting programs in the world, and I learned a lot from this class.

And so, in front of this group, I "acted" like the expert. I covered the data modeling concepts and also mentioned some of the good work done by this department. I smiled and told some jokes and made the audience feel comfortable.

After the talk, the senior Subject Matter Expert (SME for short) thanked me for mentioning his work. I was surprised he would even acknowledge me, as I barely knew much about our field. After all, he was the expert. I received several positive comments and was amazed that they believed I was the expert.

Pretending to be the expert does not mean acting cocky, overly confident, or condescending. Pretending to be the expert means thinking of the questions you might get asked and finding out the answers *before* the presentation (studying), creating a welcoming and comfortable learning environment, thinking more about the attendees than yourself, and not being afraid to acknowledge you don't know all of the answers but are willing to research and learn ("child's mind").

Now that I am older (or maybe just old), I know I am an expert within my field, but I definitely didn't know much back then. However, pretending to know what I was talking about eventually forced me to learn what I was talking about.

You will find yourself in many situations like this throughout your life. After all, whenever we do something new, we are not the expert yet.

But "fake it 'til you make it" and see what happens!

Laugh often

A police officer pulls over a semi-truck. He gets the usual license and registration, but hears strange noises coming from the trailer, so he decides to investigate. Inside, he finds 50 penguins.

"Sir, why do you have 50 penguins in your truck?" The officer asks the driver.

"Well, they're my friends, and we like to go on journeys together in my truck," the man replies.

"I'm sorry sir, but you can't just own 50 penguins. I'm afraid you're going to have to take them to the zoo."

The man agrees and drives off. The next day, the same cop pulls the truck over again, and once again hears strange noises in the trailer. He goes to check and finds the same 50 penguins.

"I thought I told you to take these penguins to the zoo yesterday!" The cop angrily tells the driver.

"I did take them to the zoo! They loved it! Today, we're going to the beach."

Laughing is so important, especially now in our crazy world. I love hearing a good joke or watching a funny movie.

I read somewhere that doctors told a man he had very little time left to live. Instead of taking lots of medicine and other treatments, he stocked up on the funniest movies he could find on VHS (this was a long time ago), and started watching them and laughing and laughing. He lived a much longer life than anyone thought.

I know laughter is the best medicine.

Not the polite laughs, but the ones that we can't control. The ones that burst out and leave us teary-eyed and full of endorphins. Don't you feel wonderful after a good laugh?

So laugh often! And make others laugh too!

Conclusion

How do you celebrate those big birthdays? You know, when you turn 21, 25, 30…or 50? I think the younger milestones involve partying with friends and planning goals, but I think we think more as we get older. 50 is "halfway over the rainbow," as our younger daughter said in one of this book's stories. After all, there are so many books written by famous people who hit 50.

We start thinking about leaving something behind. I don't mean forgetting things like a pair of glasses in a hotel room, which we may do more of as we age, but rather, leaving something to remember us when we "move on."

Maybe that's what is behind this book. But maybe not. In fact, maybe I wrote this book for us, me, and you.

For us, we get to see how much has changed in six years. It was a volatile time for the world with Covid, wars, technology, and politics.

For me, I got to see how I changed over six years. I can see that I am less the center of attention and more of a spectator or observer in some cases, admiring my family and friends. I think that is ok, too, and it must be what happens when you get older. In addition, my writing style has changed to become a bit deeper and introspective. Also, writing thoughts down makes you aware of uncertainty and clarity. Especially with the last chapter, I know these are tactics that improve my life and can improve yours.

For you, I hope you met the book's goals set in the introduction. Did you laugh out loud at least five times, smile at least 20 times, and jot down at least five messages to help you get more out of your days?

I hope so!

www.ingramcontent.com/pod-product-compliance
Lightning Source LLC
Chambersburg PA
CBHW070133080526
44586CB00015B/1673